U.S.-China Educational Exchange: Perspectives on a Growing Partnership

U.S.-China Educational Exchange: Perspectives on a Growing Partnership

EDITED BY SHEPHERD LAUGHLIN

First in a series of Global Education Research Reports

New York

IIE publications can be purchased at: www.iiebooks.org

The Institute of International Education
809 United Nations Plaza, New York, New York 10017

ISBN-13: 978-0-87206-308-2
ISBN-10: 0-87206-308-9

Library of Congress Cataloging-in-Publication Data

U.S.-China educational exchange : perspectives on a growing partnership
/ edited by Shepherd Laughlin.
    p. cm. -- (Global education research reports)
  Includes bibliographical references.
  ISBN 0-87206-307-0
 1. Educational exchanges--United States. 2. Educational
exchanges--China. 3. United States--Relations--China. 4.
China--Relations--United States. I. Laughlin, Shepherd, 1984-
  LB2376.3.C6U55 2008
  370.116'30973--dc22
                            2008041923

Cover image: Xue Song, *Dialogue with Hongren (Sea)*, 2006
    Courtesy Chinese Contemporary Gallery, New York, Beijing, London
Cover and text design: Pat Scully Design

TABLE OF CONTENTS

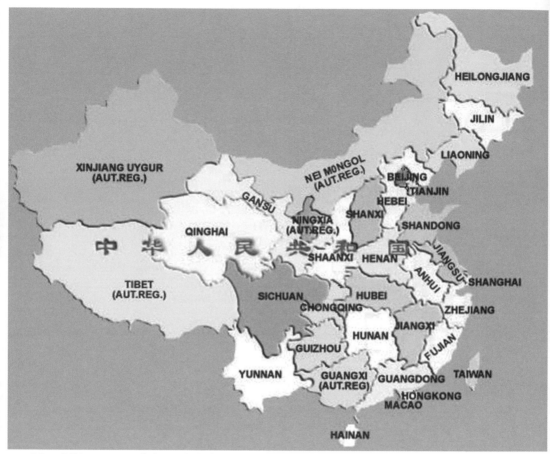

Map of China courtesy of China Scholarship Council.

FIGURES AND TABLES

Figures

Tables

FOREWORDS

BY ALLAN E. GOODMAN
INSTITUTE OF INTERNATIONAL EDUCATION

The Institute of International Education and the AIFS Foundation are pleased to present this first volume in a new series of Global Education Research Reports. Our aim is to examine some of the most pressing and under-researched topics in international education. This first report presents Chinese and American perspectives on the complex U.S.-China educational relationships, from individuals who are closely involved on the government, academic and NGO levels.

The 2008 Beijing Olympics turned the world's attention to the convergence of international athletes on China. While the athletes have gone home, increasing numbers of students and scholars are continuing to travel to Beijing and beyond for educational opportunity. We expect to see continued growth in the number of career-minded American students going to China to study, and in the number of Chinese students and scholars coming to U.S. universities.

The Institute has taken an active role in designing and implementing international education and training programs in China as well as throughout East Asia and the Pacific. We maintain a network of offices to serve the region. We support the U.S. Department of State in administering the Fulbright program in China and globally, as well as other academic exchange programs. IIE provides services to U.S. Educational Advising offices throughout the world, including more than 40 in China, and IIE offices in Hong Kong and Beijing organize U.S. higher education fairs in cities throughout East and Southeast Asia.

With this publication, the Institute and the AIFS Foundation provide a forum for individuals working in U.S.-China educational exchange to share their perspectives. Some chapters grow out of a recent roundtable discussion supported by the Fund for the Improvement of Postsecondary Education (FIPSE). We hope the wider community of policy makers, scholars and practitioners will find information to help chart the future course of their own educational exchanges with China and the world we share.

Allan E. Goodman
President & CEO, Institute of International Education

By William L. Gertz
American Institute for Foreign Study

The number of U.S. college students participating in study abroad and exchange programs in China has grown tremendously and will continue to increase provided the access to visas remains stable.

A plethora of other outbound opportunities for U.S. citizens – faculty exchanges, teaching abroad programs, internships, work programs as well as traditional summer, semester and year long study abroad programs will flourish during the coming decade.

The AIFS Foundation has seen a significant increase in the number of Chinese high school students coming to the U.S. on our Academic Year in America J-1 program to become part of a family and learn more about our country and culture. In addition, the interest in learning Mandarin among U.S. teenagers has risen dramatically, further illustrating the demand and significance of exchange between these two countries.

We have also seen growth in the number of Chinese students participating in our Summer Institute for the Gifted university programs and Au Pair in America programs. Many of these students will later enroll in U.S. universities and will return home to become the future political, business and education leaders of China.

We believe that this exchange between young people of our two nations will lead to a greater understanding of our widely different cultures and enable us to avoid future conflicts. However, our knowledge of educational opportunities in this expansive country remains extremely limited. We have therefore partnered with the Institute of International Education to produce this booklet which includes important studies by U.S. and Chinese experts and introduces some exciting exchange models.

We hope this volume, the first in a series of research reports, will be of interest to those working in the field of international education and will lead to many new creative endeavors.

William L. Gertz
President & CEO, American Institute For Foreign Study
Trustee, AIFS Foundation

INTRODUCTION

BY PEGGY BLUMENTHAL AND YANG XINYU

A View from the U.S.

BY PEGGY BLUMENTHAL, EXECUTIVE VICE PRESIDENT,
INSTITUTE OF INTERNATIONAL EDUCATION

Writing 27 years ago about the few dozen American study programs in China that I visited for the U.S.-China Education Clearinghouse, I noted "there are certain fundamental differences in the two countries' educational systems which make some frustration inevitable.... Candor, patience, and sustained effort on both sides are needed now more than ever if the new and promising relationship is to thrive."[1] It was difficult then to get an exact count on how many Americans were studying in China; estimates ranged around 500-600, compared to 6,000 students from the PRC on U.S. campuses, as reported in IIE's 1981 *Open Doors: Report on International Educational Exchange.* I wondered back then if Chinese and U.S. institutions would be willing and able to make the kinds of changes needed to expand dramatically the numbers of Americans studying in China, and whether the imbalance in academic exchange could be overcome by proactive steps on both sides.

In 1981, China's universities were still emerging from the ruins of the Cultural Revolution, with traumatized faculty, destroyed libraries, and a generation of students trying to catch up. Foreign students, clustered largely on China's eastern coast, were closely monitored and expected to focus on classroom study and language learning, rather than independent research. Free-spirited and demanding American students presented a challenge to the thinly staffed and inexperienced foreign student offices, and the highly-developed bureaucratic skills of Chinese authorities proved intensely frustrating to American students and faculty.

Today, *Open Doors* reports that close to 10,000 Americans are studying in China, in several hundred programs ranging in length from two weeks to two semesters, not counting those enrolled in degree study. The number of Chinese students on U.S. campuses has also grown dramatically, with almost 70,000 students and 10,000 scholars. The imbalance in academic exchange continues despite a tenfold increase on each side. While progress has occasionally been interrupted by political issues on both sides, especially after June 4, 1989 and September 11, 2001, the upward trend continues, driven by strong commitment on both sides at personal, institutional, and governmental levels.

Expanding its academic linkages with the U.S. is just one part of China's higher education investment/expansion plans. Today, China hosts close to 200,000 international students at several hundred institutions, with Americans making up the third largest cohort, after Koreans and Japanese. The PRC government has just announced plans to increase the number of international students to 500,000 by the year 2020. Three of China's universities are ranked among the top 100 in the *Times Higher Education QS* annual survey, and several dozen Chinese universities receive support from the government in their pursuit of world-class academic excellence. China's research labs are attracting back many foreign-trained Chinese students as well as students and faculty members from around the world. According to Simon Winchester, author of "The Man Who Loved China," the growing number of Chinese patent-holders suggests a rebirth of China's scientific dynamism that disappeared just as Western science was flourishing in the 17th century. China's strategic investment in higher education and academic exchange is supported by its rapidly expanding economy and demand for "knowledge workers" to secure a competitive advantage in the global marketplace. More than twice as many four-year engineering degrees are awarded each year in China as in America, and the Chinese rate of economic growth surpasses that of the U.S. or any European country.

China's economic and geopolitical power has expanded so rapidly in the past decade that its role as a regional and international powerhouse has gone from prediction to established fact. According to a recent Pew Global Attitudes survey, three in ten Americans believe China will surpass America as the world's leading superpower.[2] As the exchange of information and goods has increased between the United States and China, exchange of students and scholars has continued to grow at the same rapid pace.

Given the huge population difference, and the still limited higher education resources for Chinese students at home, it is unlikely that the imbalance in U.S.-China academic exchange will level off any time soon, although the level of imbalance has dropped as U.S. student flows to China have risen. More important than numerical balance is the need to insure that each side is able to benefit substantially from the process, and that students and scholars on both sides are well received and readily accommodated, able to pursue their academic goals while also benefiting their home and host campuses.

A View from China

BY YANG XINYU, DEPUTY SECRETARY GENERAL, CHINA SCHOLARSHIP COUNCIL

On June 23, 1978, Deng Xiaoping, who was reappointed as Vice President of China after the Cultural Revolution, was having discussions with the Minster of Education, Jiang Nanxiang, and the President of Tsinghua University, Liu Da, on how to escape the shadow of the Cultural Revolution, reestablish the higher education system that had almost collapsed in the past ten years, and develop China's science and technology. They reached the common understanding that the immediate need was for a large number of well trained personnel who could take up this responsibility. After ten years locked away from the outside world, Chinese universities were left far behind in the rapidly developing fields of science and technology.

Deng Xiaoping suggested that the Ministry of Education should work out a plan to send young students to study abroad, mainly in the field of science and engineering. This was the shortcut to develop China's S&T academic talents. He talked about sending thousands annually to universities in developed countries rather than just a few, despite China's poor economic situation. Deng's comments were really like a window opened and they became the guidelines on the Chinese government's policy of support for study abroad activities. The problem that followed was where to send the Chinese students, and who would like to accept them, since many institutions outside China had doubts about their academic background and foreign language ability.

On October 11, 1978, a Chinese educational delegation arrived in Washington DC, the first Chinese delegation to visit United States after the 1972 "Joint Communiqué of the United States of America and the People's Republic of China," also known as the Shanghai Communiqué. Since there was no official relationship between the two countries at the time, the delegation was "unofficial" and was headed by Zhou Peiyuan, then the President of Peking University and the Chairman of China Association of Science and Technology. The purpose of the visit was to discuss student exchange with U.S. authorities. The delegation was well received by its counterparts, several of whom had participated in a similar "unofficial" visit to Beijing in summer of 1978. The U.S. team was headed by Dr. Richard Atkinson, Director of the National Science Foundation, and the members included Dr. Frank Press, the Science Advisor to the President and officials from the White House, Department of State and National Science Foundation.

After several days' discussion, an unofficial, oral "memorandum of understanding" was reached: the Chinese side would send 500-700 students and scholars to study in the American institutions, and the U.S. side would send about 50 American students to China. Both sides agreed to encourage direct contact between universities, research institutes and scholars. According to this "oral MOU," the first 52 visiting Chinese scholars arrived in the United States via Paris on December 26, 1978, right before the formal establishment of diplomatic relations between China and the United States. Liu Baicheng, leader of the 52 Chinese scholars, and now fellow of Chinese Academy of Sciences, recalled his experience: "When we arrived at New York JFK airport and facing a big group of media, I read a prepared note on behalf of the rest: 'China and the United States are great nations with great people. We are here not only to learn science and technology but also for the friendship of the two people.'" The arrival of these 52 scholars to the United States turned a new page of China's opening up to the outside world, and was a milestone for Chinese scholars studying overseas.

But sending visiting scholars abroad was not what Deng Xiaoping really meant. He was thinking about sending young students to earn higher degrees and return with knowledge and experiences to contribute to the development of the nation. In recognition of the fact that foreign institutions had no idea of the quality of Chinese students and their level of English, Dr. Tsung-Dao Lee, the Chinese-American Nobel Laureate, initiated a program named "China-U.S. Physics Examination and Application." He lobbied a number of prestigious U.S. universities, persuading them to provide scholarships to Chinese students for graduate study, mainly at the PhD level. Since there were no TOFEL or GRE tests in China at the time, these awards were based on the results of a test specially designed by several U.S. universities to check the academic and English level of Chinese students. A year later, Dr. Ray Wu, a Chinese-American professor at Cornell University, proposed a similar program on biological science (CUSBEA 1982-1989) to the Chinese government and selected students of biological sciences to send to study at U.S. universities. From these programs, U.S. universities gradually recognized the quality of Chinese students. Today, there are over 80,000 Chinese students studying at U.S. universities, and China is the second most common place of origin of all the international graduate students in U.S. universities, right after India.

After 30 years of fast economic growth, more and more families in China can afford to support their children's pursuit of overseas studies. According to statistics published by the Chinese Ministry of Education, from 1978 to 2007 over 1 million (1.27 million) Chinese students studied abroad, over a quarter million (0.31 million) returned to China, and over half a million (0.65 million) were undertaking study or research in higher education institutions or research institutes in over 100 countries all around the world. The returned students and scholars play a very important role in China's economic and social development. I attended the ceremony of the 25th anniversary of CUSBEA on July 25, 2007 and was so impressed by the achievements of the alumni and how greatly this program has contributed to bio-science research in China. When I asked for her comments on the government sending young students for graduate study overseas, Dr. Gu Xiaocheng, a very respected professor at Peking University and the main administrator of CUSBEA, said to me: "If there is any Chinese who could win the Nobel Price in bio-science, it must be one of the CUSBEA alumni!"

Today, China-U.S. educational exchange and cooperation comes in all forms:

student and scholar exchanges, joint teaching and research programs, co-supervising graduate students, summer/winter camps for pre-college students. The nature of the exchange is very much mutually beneficial. The U.S. Fulbright Program is now named U.S.-China Fulbright Program: in 2004, the funding model of the program was changed from being solely supported by the U.S. government to being equally funded by both governments, and the number of Chinese scholars under this program doubled.

In recent years, China has become a leading destination country for international education. Chinese universities attract many students from neighboring countries, especially East Asian countries. According to data collected by the China Scholarship Council, in 2007 there were 195,503 international students studying in 544 higher education institutions in 31 provinces and autonomous regions in China. Among them, 14,758 students were from the United States. The U.S. ranks number 3 in terms of the number of its students in Chinese universities, after Korea (64,481) and Japan (18,640). To be internationally recognized, Chinese universities have tried very hard to attract international students, and have taken many measures, including attending international education exhibitions, providing scholarships, offering courses in English, and improving the living and study conditions of international students. It is also nice to see that more U.S. students in Chinese universities are taking degree courses, even though a larger number still comes to China for short-term language and culture study.

U.S. universities are always the number one choice for young Chinese students looking for overseas study opportunities, and this will continue to be true. Among the 4,000 PhD students supported by the China Scholarship Council in 2007, half chose to study in U.S. universities. I expect to see more U.S. students studying in China in the coming years, and continued deepening of academic ties between our two countries.

NOTES

[1] Peggy Blumenthal, *American Study Programs in China: An Interim Report Card* (Washington, DC: US-China Education Clearinghouse: A joint project of NAFSA and the CSCPRC, October 1981).

[2] Meg Bortin, "Global Image of U.S. Improves Slightly," *The New York Times*, July 13, 2008. Available online: http://www.nytimes.com/2008/06/13/world/13pew.html.

Chapter One

TRENDS AND MODELS OF ACADEMIC EXCHANGE BETWEEN CHINA AND THE U.S.

BY SHEPHERD LAUGHLIN, INSTITUTE OF INTERNATIONAL EDUCATION

As models for international education have proliferated in recent years, the overall picture has become both more exciting and more confusing. Gaining a grasp of the situation can be even more difficult in the case of China, whose domestic education system has undergone rapid restructuring along with internationalization. In the context of China's increased role in globalization, U.S. administrators and educators feel compelled to develop programs in China and linkages with Chinese institutions.

Scholars are increasingly investigating the growth of China's higher education system and the role that Chinese academics returning from abroad play in the development of Chinese higher education and society. However, surprisingly little has been written on U.S.-China exchange, despite enormous changes to this exchange relationship within the last few years.

This chapter seeks to describe current models of educational exchange, place them in the context of rising U.S. student interest in China and the Chinese language, and offer examples of the range of locations and fields of study currently available to U.S. students. First, it examines trends in educational exchange and student mobility between the U.S. and China. Next, it examines the growing interest in Chinese language study, an indication of growing student interest in this part of the world. It then identifies five linkage models: study abroad, joint degree programs, research partnerships, branch campuses, and Confucius Institutes.

Explanations of each model are followed by a few notable program examples. These are not meant to highlight best practices or to be an exhaustive list, but instead are intended to illustrate each of these linkage models in action. They have been selected to show that each different model can accommodate a wide range of programs. Variation occurs across the type of institution offering the program (community colleges and 4-year institutions), field of study (science and technology and humanities), geographic location, and other factors.

Increasing Openness in China's Education Sector

Study abroad to China from the U.S. has grown from a virtual standstill thirty years ago to a veritable industry that today involves nearly ten thousand American participants per year. Exchange activities between China and the United States resumed in 1979 after grinding to a halt at the height of the Cold War. As China began its period of economic reform and opening up, American students were welcomed to study in China. Chinese students also quickly became a more common sight on U.S. college campuses. In 1985, President Reagan and Chinese President Li Xiannian signed an agreement "… to provide opportunities for cooperation and exchange in educational fields based on equality, reciprocity, and mutual benefit."[1] The liberalization of the education sector, which accompanied China's entry into the World Trade Organization in 2001, has permitted more students from outside China to enter the Chinese educational system. New international academic exchange programs and joint research initiatives are growing rapidly in number and scope.[2]

FIGURE 1.1 TOP TEN COUNTRIES SENDING STUDENTS TO CHINA, 2006

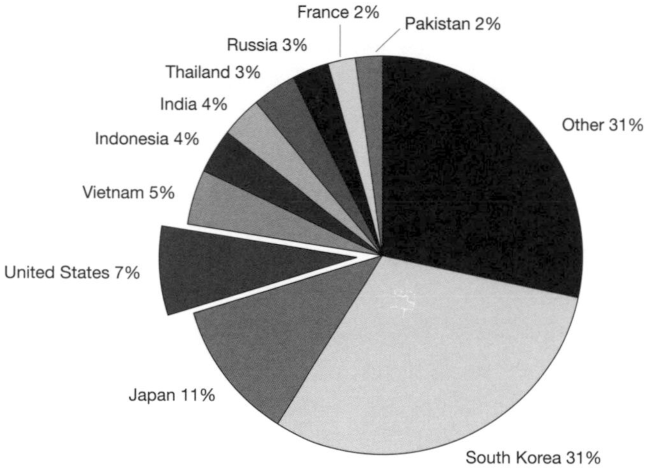

Source: *Atlas of International Student Mobility*, "Destinations: China (2006)." Available online: http://www.atlas.iienetwork.org/?p=53467.

International students from countries around the world have increasingly sought out China as a study destination in recent years. China is now ranked fifth as a destination country for international students behind the U.S., the United Kingdom, France and Germany, placing it far above any other developing country.[3] Six percent of all internationally mobile students worldwide choose to study in China, and a total of 162,695 international students studied at Chinese universities in 2006. South Korea sent the greatest proportion of these students, sending 31 percent of the total, and Japan was a distant second at 11 percent. The U.S. is ranked as the third largest sending country and the largest non-Asian sending country, sending 7 percent of all international students studying in China. Other key sending countries include Vietnam, Indonesia, India, Thailand, Russia, France, and Pakistan.[4]

Chapter One | Shepherd Laughlin
TRENDS AND MODELS OF ACADEMIC EXCHANGE BETWEEN CHINA AND THE U.S.

Growth in U.S. Study Abroad to China

In recent years China has become increasingly popular as a destination country for American study abroad students. While the volume of students going to China is low compared to Chinese flows into the U.S., the rate at which it has increased is staggering: 1,396 Americans studied in China in 1995/96 and 8,830 did in 2005/06, a 533% increase in ten years, according to IIE's *Open Doors Report on International Educational Exchange.*[5] China is now the seventh most popular destination for American students, attracting 4.0% of all study abroad students, compared to 1.6% in 1995/96. China's entry into the WTO in 2001 and the parallel liberalization of its education sector, along with increasing awareness among U.S. students of China's increasing political and economic clout, surely contributed to this astonishing growth. The dramatic drop in numbers in 2003 is the result of the impact of the SARS epidemic, when many American study abroad programs to China were temporarily suspended. Afterwards, study abroad programs quickly resumed in China, and since then their growth has rebounded with great speed.

FIGURE 1.2 NUMBER OF AMERICAN STUDENTS STUDYING IN CHINA, 1995/96-2005/06

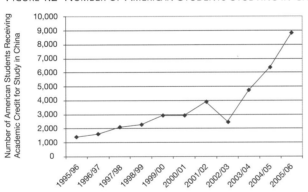

Source: Rajika Bhandari and Patricia Chow, *Open Doors 2007: Report on International Educational Exchange* (New York: Institute of International Education, 2007). Older data is compiled from previous annual *Open Doors* reports.

China as a Sending Country

Since 1985/86, China has been among the top places of origin sending students to the United States.

IIE/AIFS Foundation Global Education Research Reports
U.S.-CHINA EDUCATIONAL EXCHANGE: PERSPECTIVES ON A GROWING PARTNERSHIP

3

FIGURE 1.3 TRENDS IN LEADING PLACES OF ORIGIN, 1985/86 TO 2005/06

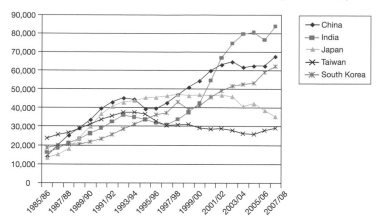

Source: Rajika Bhandari and Patricia Chow, *Open Doors 2007: Report on International Educational Exchange* (New York: Institute of International Education, 2007). Older data is compiled from previous annual *Open Doors* reports.

As of 2006/07, the most recent year for which *Open Doors* data are available, 67,723 Chinese students were studying on U.S. campuses. This represents a record-high, following a slight post-9/11 decline. Chinese students make up 11.6% of the total international student population in the U.S., and increased 8.2% from the previous year.

FIGURE 1.4 CHINESE STUDENTS IN THE UNITED STATES BY ACADEMIC LEVEL, 1989/90-2006/07

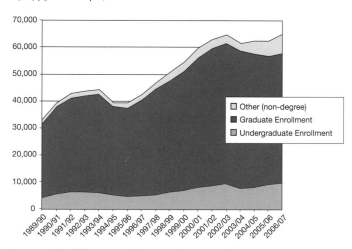

Source: Rajika Bhandari and Patricia Chow, *Open Doors 2007: Report on International Educational Exchange* (New York: Institute of International Education, 2007). Older data is compiled from previous annual *Open Doors* reports. Data for 1992/93 is not available, and is estimated for the purpose of this figure.

Although a complete *Open Doors* report and analysis for the 2007/08 academic year are not yet available, IIE conducted a joint snapshot survey in Fall 2007 along with seven other higher education associations, with 700 U.S. campuses responding. This survey reported further increases in enrollments from China. More institutions reported increases than declines in the number of students from China, with 53% reporting increases, 10% reporting declines, and the rest reporting level enrollments.

FIGURE 1.5 GROWTH IN STUDENTS AND SCHOLARS FROM CHINA TO THE U.S., 1985/86-2006/07

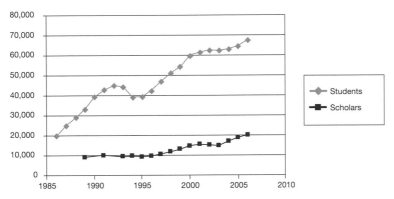

Source: Rajika Bhandari and Patricia Chow, *Open Doors 2007: Report on International Educational Exchange* (New York: Institute of International Education, 2007). Older data is compiled from previous annual *Open Doors* reports. Scholars were not counted prior to 1989, and were not counted in 1990 or 1992.

The number of Chinese scholars teaching and doing research at U.S. colleges and universities has followed a similar general upward trend in recent years. China is by far the largest sending country for foreign scholars (faculty members and visiting lecturers and researchers). With 20,149 Chinese scholars in the U.S. in 2006/07, China sends more than twice as many scholars to the U.S. as South Korea, the second largest sending country with 9,291 scholars in the U.S. in the same year. [6]

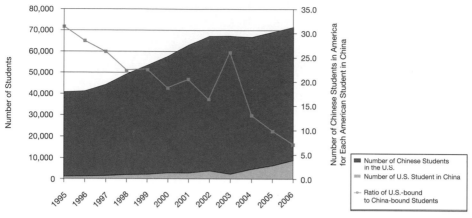

FIGURE 1.6 TRENDS IN SINO-AMERICAN ACADEMIC EXCHANGE, 1995/96-2005/06

Source: Rajika Bhandari and Patricia Chow, *Open Doors 2007: Report on International Educational Exchange* (New York: Institute of International Education, 2007). Older data is compiled from previous annual *Open Doors* reports.

In the figure above, one can see that the growth in educational exchange between the United States and China has been remarkable in several respects. There have been increases in absolute numbers in both directions of exchange, and at the same time a dramatic change in the ratio of U.S.-bound to China-bound students. In 1995/96, there were 31 Chinese students in the U.S. for every U.S. student in China; by 2005/06, there were seven. The significant change in this ratio is all the more notable since it took place even in the context of increased numbers of Chinese students studying in the U.S., indicating an even greater increase in China-bound American students.

Chinese Language Programs at U.S. Higher Education Institutions

Student interest in China has risen dramatically in the past decade. One clear way to gauge interest in China is through the growth in Chinese language programs stateside. Not surprisingly, Chinese language instruction at the post-secondary level has also seen tremendous growth in the past decade. According to a report issued by the Modern Language Association, Chinese enrollments between 2002 and 2006 grew 51%, second only to percentage growth in Arabic enrollments at 127%.[7] This follows a 20% increase in Chinese programs from 1998 to 2002. In absolute terms, Chinese gained 5,697 student enrollments between 1998 and 2002, and an additional 17,429 between 2002 and 2006. As of fall 2006, total enrollment in Chinese language courses at the postsecondary level stood at 51,582, making Chinese the second most commonly studied non-European foreign language, after Japanese. Chinese is now the sixth most commonly studied foreign language in the U.S. (not counting American Sign Language).

TABLE 1.1 FALL 2002 AND 2006 LANGUAGE COURSE ENROLLMENTS IN U.S. INSTITUTIONS OF HIGHER EDUCATION (LANGUAGES IN DESCENDING ORDER OF 2006 TOTALS)

	2002	2006	Percent Change
Spanish	746,267	822,985	10.3
French	201,979	206,426	2.2
German	91,100	94,264	3.5
American Sign Language	60,781	78,829	29.7
Italian	63,899	78,368	22.6
Japanese	52,238	66,605	27.5
Chinese	34,153	51,582	51
Latin	29,841	32,191	7.9
Russian	23,921	24,845	3.9
Arabic	10,584	23,974	126.5
Greek, Ancient	20,376	22,849	12.1
Hebrew, Biblical	14,183	14,140	-0.3
Portuguese	8,385	10,267	22.4
Hebrew, Modern	8,619	9,612	11.5
Korean	5,211	7,145	37.1
Other languages	25,716	33,728	31.2
Total	1,397,253	1,577,810	12.9

Source: Furman and others, MLA, available online:
http://www.mla.org/pdf/06enrollmentsurvey_final.pdf.

Ratios of beginning to advanced enrollment in all languages are dramatic, with five beginning level Spanish students for every one advanced level student, for example. Interestingly, despite the difficulty of Chinese, the ratio is about the same: 4.5 beginning students for every one advanced student. For Arabic, in contrast, the ratio is 8:1. This indicates that Chinese departments are enrolling advanced students at a level comparable to Romance language departments. However, advanced level courses in each language may not represent a comparable degree of fluency.

TABLE 1.2 GROWTH IN CHINESE LANGUAGE ENROLLMENTS IN THE U.S., 1960-2006

Year	Students
1960	1,844
1968	5,061
1980	11,366
1986	16,891
1990	19,490
1995	26,471
1998	28,456
2002	34,153
2006	51,582

Source: Furman and others, MLA, available online:
http://www.mla.org/pdf/06enrollmentsurvey_final.pdf.

IIE/AIFS Foundation Global Education Research Reports
U.S.-CHINA EDUCATIONAL EXCHANGE: PERSPECTIVES ON A GROWING PARTNERSHIP

7

Chinese language instruction in the U.S. is largely focused on Mandarin, the 'official' dialect of China most commonly spoken in Beijing and northern China. Enrollments in other languages and dialects of China, including Cantonese, Uyghur, Mongolian, Tibetan, and Classical Chinese, have generally increased since 2002, but remain extremely low in comparison to Mandarin, according to the MLA survey.

In the context of increasing interest from students and institutions, models of U.S.-China academic exchange have proliferated in recent years. We now turn to an exploration of five exchange models: study abroad, joint degree programs, research partnerships, branch campuses and Confucius Institutes.

Study Abroad: Short-term and Long-term Programs

Study abroad programs in China for American students vary greatly in length, location and field of study. They are offered by American universities and third-party providers, often with a Chinese institution serving as a host campus and handling administrative issues, but not often with an equal role in planning the curriculum. These programs take place most often in Beijing and Shanghai, but also exist in other cities throughout China. Many of these programs, although they are managed by only one U.S. university, may accept students from any U.S. university or even universities overseas.

IIE's directories of study abroad programs, *IIEPassport: Short-Term Study Abroad* and *IIEPassport: Academic Year Abroad*, have a combined total listing of over 8,000 study abroad programs in the 2008/09 edition. These directories have been published since 1950 and 1971, respectively. Programs listed in the *IIEPassport* directories offer a broad look at study abroad programs in China, including both short-term programs conducted mostly in the summer months and long-term semester- or academic year-length programs. The overwhelming majority of these programs are open to all students, with no preference that students be enrolled in the sponsoring institution.

Despite the many programs listed in *IIEPassport* and open to all students, most students who study abroad do so through programs affiliated with their home institutions. *Open Doors* reports that 72 percent of U.S. study abroad students went abroad through programs sponsored solely by their own institutions.[8] This figure is likely to be lower in the case of China, since fewer schools have established their own programs there than in European countries. Students wishing to go to China, still considered a non-traditional study abroad destination, are more likely to have to look beyond what their own institutions offer for appropriate program options than are students going to Western Europe. Therefore, looking at the programs in *IIEPassport* provides a reasonably clear picture of the range of programs available in China, especially from the perspective of students whose institutions have not yet developed extensive programs in China. The analysis that follows is based on data from the *IIEPassport* directories.[9] The program listings also appear online at www.iiepassport.org.

IIEPassport contains 132 program listings for short-term programs and 92 program listings for long-term programs in China. Short-term study abroad programs, defined for the purposes of this study as any program lasting less than a semester, are organized by American universities and colleges and involve collaboration with a Chinese host institution to a greater or lesser extent. They are often designed at the American institution and carried out in China by American faculty, sometimes with the assistance of local Chinese faculty. Long-term study abroad programs are defined as either semester- or academic year-length study programs. Long-term programs are also often collaborative projects between Chinese and U.S. institutions and faculty.

Trends in program location vary considerably between short-term and long-term programs. More than half of long-term programs in *IIEPassport* are offered in Beijing or Shanghai, and a few are located in second-tier cities and inland cities such as Chengdu, Chongqing, Xi'an and Guilin. Relatively few programs are offered in multiple cities or in more than one city through the course of the academic year. In contrast, short-term study programs are offered in more diverse locales. Less than half of these programs take place in Beijing and Shanghai, more than a third of them are offered in multiple cities, and programs are available in less commonly visited areas such as Inner Mongolia and Xinjiang Province.

FIGURE 1.7 PROGRAM LOCATION OF SHORT TERM AND ACADEMIC YEAR PROGRAMS IN CHINA

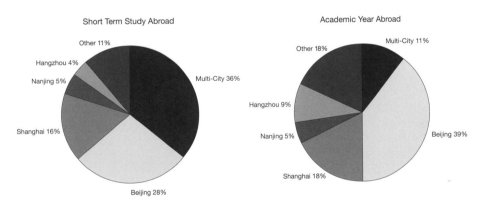

Data Source: O'Sullivan, *IIEPassport*.

Study abroad programs in China cover diverse fields of study. Some programs include courses in a full range of humanities disciplines, and some are in specialized fields, most commonly Chinese language and Chinese studies and business. Very few programs focus on science and technology, and those that do usually include a language component and emphasize the social and cultural context of science rather than scientific knowledge or scientific research itself.

Long-term programs are overwhelmingly Chinese language programs or humanities programs with a Chinese studies component. Beyond these, programs with a primary emphasis on business and management or political science, often also including a language component, make up most of the rest of the programs. There are also long-term programs in other specialized fields such as musical composition and physical education.

The most popular short-term programs are in Chinese language and culture, followed by business-related subjects and then more specialized programs in fields such as visual arts, martial arts, traditional Chinese medicine, urban planning and design, archaeology and botany. Internship and volunteer opportunities are also available. Short-term business programs are much more common than long-term business programs. There are very few short-term programs in science, engineering, mathematics and technology (STEM) fields.

FIGURE 1.8 FIELD OF STUDY OF SHORT-TERM AND LONG-TERM PROGRAMS IN CHINA

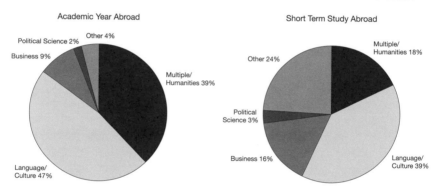

Data Source: O'Sullivan, *IIEPassport*.

Some prior knowledge of Mandarin is required for many of these programs. Students without knowledge of Chinese can enroll in language intensive programs and then enter more advanced studies. Some American universities require a demonstrated fluency (academic coursework at the home institution) or waiver exams as a condition for program participation. Many American universities offer the option of direct enrollment in Chinese universities, especially elite universities such as Peking University, and these institutions often have their own (often more rigorous) language requirements for participation.

Short-term Study Abroad Program Examples

Indiana University – Purdue University Indianapolis

China Law Summer Program
http://indylaw.indiana.edu/programs/china[10]

This university is one of the relatively few institutions that provide short-term faculty-led programs to law students. The program consists of four weeks of morning classes on the Chinese legal system and domestic law as it relates to the economy, as well as site visits to significant Chinese legal entities, such as the National People's Congress, the Supreme People's Court, the Haidian District Court, arbitration agencies, and a "major Chinese law firm." Sightseeing is included, and the course counts for five credit hours.

Harvard University

Harvard Beijing Academy
www.summer.harvard.edu/2008/programs/abroad/beijing

This program covers the most common subject matter for summer faculty-led programs, Chinese language and culture, but is atypical in duration and intensity. Students must abide by a pledge to speak only Mandarin Chinese for the duration of the program. Students must learn a full year of university Chinese at any of four levels in a total of nine weeks. The fifth week of the program is devoted to social study, which goes toward producing a written report in Chinese. The program is supplemented with tourist visits, social events and lectures.

University of Maryland

Dissecting Martial Arts
www.international.umd.edu/studyabroad/4190

This program, which lasts for two weeks during the winter break and is based in Shanghai, provides students experiences with martial arts masters, practitioners and scholars at all skill levels. The program combines instruction in martial arts with the academic goal of understanding the cultural and social traditions of martial arts and their influence on contemporary life.

Northwestern University

China Science and Engineering Research Summer Program
http://www.northwestern.edu/studyabroad/programs/profiles/asia/China

Very few study abroad programs in China focus on STEM fields, and short-term faculty led programs generally do not focus only on these fields. This program, hosted by Tsinghua University and Capital Medical University, offers three distinct courses: Emerging Legal and Economic Structures, Public Health in China, and Science and Engineering Research. Each of these courses is combined with Chinese language study and site visits.

Long-term Study Abroad Program Examples

<u>SUNY Buffalo</u>

Beijing University of Technology
http://inted.oie.buffalo.edu/studyabroad/all.asp

The university's School of Engineering and Applied Sciences has an exchange program with Beijing University of Technology. American students have the option to either immerse themselves in an intensive Chinese language program or, if they already possess intermediate or proficient knowledge of Chinese, they can enroll into any courses offered at the Beijing University of Technology. The exchange program includes an informal English-teaching option in which American students tutor and teach English to their Chinese peers for a small monetary compensation. SUNY Buffalo also offers several other programs in China.

<u>College of Lake County</u>

Semester Abroad in Xi'an, China
www.clcillinois.edu/depts/socdv/studyabroad/studyAbroad.asp

The College of Lake County, a community college in the Chicago area, is one of the few community colleges to offer its own semester-length study program in China. The study abroad program is one aspect of a new East Asian Studies program made possible through a Title VI-A grant from the U.S. Department of Education. Through a partnership with Xi'an International University, CLC students take Chinese language classes, as well as classes taught in English and taken along with Chinese students. These include economics, Chinese culture and society, and American literature and history. One CLC faculty member teaches courses as part of the program, along with other international faculty. Students live in university dormitories with Chinese and other international students.

<u>New York University</u>

NYU in Shanghai
www.nyu.edu/studyabroad/shanghai

NYU in Shanghai offers academic programs during the fall and spring semesters. A variety of liberal arts courses examine modern Chinese culture and society through the lenses of comparative literature, history, journalism and economics. Because the emphasis is on maximizing the cross-cultural experience, students from the partner university, East China Normal University, participate in NYU courses as well. Experienced academics and scholars, curators and filmmakers, and accomplished industry leaders instruct each content course in English.

Pacific Lutheran University

Continuity and Change in an Emerging World Power
www.plu.edu/wangcenter/study-away/sichuan-university.html

PLU's program at Sichuan University in Chengdu is one of the few semester-length programs based in inland China. This semester-length program is supplemented by study tours in Beijing, Xi'an and Tibet. All students are required to take "Intensive Chinese Language," "Chinese Culture and Society" and "Western China: The Rural and Minority Experience." Other elective courses include business, political science and calligraphy. A "service learning" component sends students to use their English skills to students and teachers at local schools.

Yale University-Peking University

Joint Undergraduate Program in Beijing
www.yale.edu/iefp/pku-yale

Yale College students and honor students at Peking University study and live together on the campus in Beijing as part of this program. The Yale College students selected for the program take a full course load taught in English by Yale and Peking University faculty and receive full Yale credit toward their degrees. The Chinese students generally participate in the Yuanpei program at Peking University, an opportunity to spend two years taking liberal education courses before deciding on a major field of study. The Chinese students receive Peking University credit for this program, so both Chinese and American participants only earn credit from their home institutions. The program is open to American students with no Chinese language skills as well as to students who speak Chinese. All Yale students study Chinese language as part of the program, and students who are already fluent have the option of direct enrollment at Peking University.

Study Abroad Offered Through Third-Party Providers

Many smaller universities may not offer international programs specifically in Asia, but want to provide their students with opportunities for global exposure. They may lack the resources to develop their own quality programs. Third-party providers and organizations help these universities organize study tours, internship placements for credit, and direct enrollment at Chinese institutions. Individual students may also be unable to find university programs that meet their specific needs, and outside providers may offer a more individualized experience or a wider range of options.

Some companies, such as EducAsian, Abroad China, Inc. and Global Exchange Education Center operate exclusively in China, whereas others including CET Academic Programs, the American Institute For Foreign Study (AIFS), and the Council for International Educational Exchange (CIEE) offer programs in many countries around the globe. Many programs operated through third-parties are short-term summer programs, but some longer programs and placement opportunities exist as well.

Abroad China, Inc.

www.abroadchina.net

Abroad China specializes in internship programs, volunteer opportunities and study tours. For the internship program, Abroad China places each intern individually depending on field of interest and qualifications, and offers summer programs for students, long-term placement for young professionals, and internships and language courses for MBA students. The company also offers customized study tours for universities and organizations, combining visits to historical sites and companies with lectures and research projects. The company emphasizes its flexibility, adaptability, and connections to local resources.

American Institute for Foreign Study (AIFS)

www.aifsabroad.com

China is one of 16 countries in which AIFS operates college study abroad programs. AIFS has a multi-site summer program in Beijing, Nanjing and Shanghai. The program offers Mandarin study, but no previous language experience is required for participation. AIFS also offers semester and year-length programs at Nanjing University, which combine Chinese language study at all levels with content courses taught in English.

Council for International Educational Exchange (CIEE)

www.ciee.org

CIEE, a non-governmental international education organization founded in 1947, administers approximately 104 study abroad programs in over 35 host countries and additional teaching programs in Chile, China, Spain, and Thailand. Among these are eight China programs located in Beijing, Shanghai and Nanjing. Most focus on Chinese language, with options for intensive, beginning, and advanced studies. Some programs include supplementary site visits in Sichuan and Yunnan provinces, and may include programs in non-language topics such as business and minority nationality studies.

EducAsian

www.educasian.com

EducAsian has operated study abroad programs in China since 1992, and offers Mandarin language, business programs, martial arts classes, university direct enrollment assistance, home stays, and high school and "gap year" programs. Many of these programs are accredited through the State University of New York, and EducAsian also coordinates the Global MBA Residency in Shanghai program for Georgetown University.

Joint Degree Programs

Models for joint degree programs tend to be idiosyncratic. The European University Association asserts that there is no common definition of 'joint degree' in use at this time, either explicitly or implicitly. However, one working definition of a transnational joint degree is "an arrangement whereby providers in different countries collaborate to offer a program for which a student receives a qualification from each provider or a joint award from the collaborating providers. It is a degree which is cosponsored with other institutions."[11]

The number of American universities and colleges offering joint degree programs with Chinese counterparts has been increasing since the late 1990s. Today, with more flexible Chinese government educational policies, these programs are becoming increasingly popular, as logistical costs decrease. In many cases, joint degree programs have built upon existing successful exchange partnerships. Although a variety of American partners including second-tier and technical universities have been involved in these programs, the Chinese counterparts are in many cases limited to the elite institutions that receive funding from Project 985, the major Chinese government higher education funding initiative whose goal is to produce first-rate, internationally competitive Chinese universities. Program content is diverse, from business to humanities to the sciences.

Joint degrees and branch campuses often encounter problems beyond those of regular study abroad programs as a result of the intense institutional collaboration that joint degrees necessitate. Researchers at Washburn University have offered five possible roadblocks to the establishment of such programs:

1. The two countries [China and the U.S.] share drastically different views of the purpose of college education and what [role] general education serves in higher education.

2. Correlated courses presents [sic] a challenge. Correlated courses are viewed by China as a minor extension of the specialty area. A Chinese science degree in CS&T typically requires correlated courses only in the natural sciences. The U.S. uses correlated courses to broaden the students' intellectual horizons by covering different subjects.

3. A major motivation for Chinese students to come to the U.S. is to improve their English language skills. This entails that … they still need to take additional English courses in a U.S. institute to boost their language skills.

4. Some minor gaps in the major courses are inevitable.

5. For courses that have the same title and description, what factors are used for comparison to determine equivalency? … If a course is found not to be equivalent, how is this resolved?[12]

So, differences in educational philosophy, the logistics of curricular coordination and the language can hamper efforts to develop these programs. Political factors in the United States also must be considered in this context. For example, an attempt by the State University of New York to launch an ambitious dual degree program had to be reformulated into a much smaller dual degree partnership after concerns were raised by U.S. immigration authorities, and SUNY administrators worried about resistance from the New York legislature to funding the large-scale education of Chinese citizens.[13] Nevertheless, several productive joint degree programs have been established with Chinese universities, and many more are in the planning stages.

American Association of State Colleges and Universities (AASCU) and China Center for International Education Exchange (CCIEE)

1-2-1 Joint Degree Program, www.cciee121.com

Fourteen American universities participate in this program designed to offer joint bachelor's degrees from an American and Chinese university to Chinese undergraduate students. At present there is no opportunity for American students to study in China as part of this program. Participating universities include: Northern Arizona University, Ball State University, George Mason University, Troy State University, the University of North Carolina at Pembroke, and many others. More than 50 Chinese universities now participate, including Nanjing Normal University, Shanghai International Studies University, Guangxi Teachers Education College, and Beijing Teachers University. Chinese students complete their freshman year at a Chinese university, spend their sophomore and junior years at a U.S. university, and finish with their senior year at the Chinese university. This structure addresses concerns of both governments involved that Chinese students might attempt to stay in the U.S. after completing their joint degrees.

University of Maryland and Nanjing Normal University

Joint Education Program, www.mcj.umd.edu/nnu/index.asp

The University of Maryland and Nanjing Normal University of China offer a joint master's degree in Criminal Justice. Five faculty members from the University of Maryland teach five master's degree courses at Nanjing Normal University. The program incorporates various e-learning components, and courses include criminology, jurisprudence and international law. The program is available only to Chinese students, and includes a practical training component that takes place in the United States.

Simon Fraser University (Canada) and Zhejiang University

> Dual Degree Program in Canada and China,
> www.cs.sfu.ca/undergrad/prospective/ddp/index.php
>
> This program offers a unique dual degree model in the key field of computing science, giving Canadian and Chinese students (or international students at SFU) the opportunity to earn a Bachelor of Science degree from both participating universities. Canadian students must also become proficient in Mandarin. The program lasts five years, and has a 1-2-2 structure for SFU students: first year at SFU, the next two years at ZU, and the final two years back at SFU. While the 1-2-1 degree structure is fairly common for Chinese students in the United States, no American university yet offers such a model to American students wishing to study in China, which makes the SFU program an interesting example.

Research Partnerships

Research partnerships are a relatively common way for American universities to collaborate with China. They may arise organically as a result of the research interests of specific academic departments, and they may be formal top-down agreements brokered by university administrators that link researchers in similar departments or with similar interests. One model followed by Yale, Arizona State University and George Mason University involves the coordination of diverse China-related research efforts across campus under an institutionalized university-wide China coordinator or office. These loosely organized umbrella groups for China-related activities seem to reflect a concerted effort from the administration at these schools to reach out specifically to China.

Yale University

> Multiple research partnerships, http://world.yale.edu/regions/east_asia.html
>
> Yale maintains a geographically extensive and academically diverse set of research partnerships and collaborations with Chinese institutions. The Yale-China Association, a non-profit organization separate from Yale, promotes close interaction among individuals and sustained, long-term relationships with Chinese partner institutions and organizations designed to build Chinese institutional capacity. Yale schools involved in research collaboration include the School of Epidemiology and Public Health, the School of Forestry and Environmental Studies, and the School of Medicine, the Graduate School of Arts and Sciences, and others. Yale's President Richard Levin is actively involved in spearheading these efforts, and in bringing institutional coherence to the many China-related projects across Yale.[14]

John Hopkins University and Tsinghua University

> Joint Center for Biomedical Engineering Research, www.bme.jhu.edu

John Hopkins University and Tsinghua University have established Tsinghua-Johns Hopkins Joint Center for Biomedical Engineering Research with the goal of building a high-level international academic platform that combines engineering and life science. The Center carries out research in such biomedical engineering frontier areas as neural engineering, medical imaging, and tissue engineering. It also promotes graduate student and faculty exchanges, and organizes bilateral academic symposia.[15]

Arizona State University

Multiple projects under China Initiatives and Special Projects Office (CISPO), www.asu.edu/chinainitiatives

Arizona State University faculty are doing research in eight different locations in China in many different fields. One example is a close research and faculty exchange relationship between ASU and Peking University's Center for the Study of Ancient Chinese History. ASU is also working to develop a partnership with Yunnan University in Kunming, in China's mountainous southwest, which may soon result in a new Master in American Studies degree at Yunnan University. In Inner Mongolia, ASU faculty have worked with colleagues at the Institute of Botany in the Chinese Academy of Sciences for the past few years on biodiversity and ecosystem functioning. Their combined aim is to provide an ecological basis for understanding and achieving grassland sustainability. These diverse activities are grouped together under the China Initiatives and Special Projects Office (CISPO), and ASU President Michael Crow is actively involved with these activities at the administrative level. ASU's W.P. Carey School of Business also operates an executive MBA program in Shanghai.

Branch Campuses

There are several American branch campuses currently operating in China. These institutions require a Chinese partner, but the degree of partnership varies depending on the individual case. The most recognized are the Hopkins-Nanjing Center and the Missouri State University Branch Campus at Liaoning Normal University.[16] Many other universities have begun the process of establishing branch campuses, but are currently waiting for approval from the Chinese government, as in the case of the University of Montana and Kean University, or have scaled back their plans for branch campuses to plans for joint degree programs, as in the case of the SUNY system.[17] Academic models for these institutions are very individualized, and with so few branch campuses currently in existence, it is near impossible to discern meaningful trends in curricular models. Instead, individual models will be discussed in the examples below.

American and British branch campuses, both existing and planned, are located in industrial and manufacturing provinces of eastern China, notably Zhejiang and

Jiangsu provinces, both of which border Shanghai. Zhejiang province, south and west of Shanghai, is host to the existing University of Nottingham campus in Ningbo, as well as the hypothetical Kean University campus in Wenzhou. The Hopkins-Nanjing Center is in Nanjing, the capital and largest city of Jiangsu province, and so is the China campus of New York Institute of Technology. Missouri State University operates a branch campus in Dalian, a major city in the northeastern province of Liaoning. An exception is the Xi'an Jiaotong-Liverpool University, located in Shaanxi province, far inland from these coastal industrial centers.

Some Chinese students choose branch campuses over study abroad out of fear that being away from home for so long will undermine personal connections at home, and thus make it more difficult to find a job after their return from the United States.[18] The option of the branch campus at least theoretically combines American-style study and pedagogy in English with the advantage of maintaining personal connections to the local job market. However, some administrators have recently questioned the extent to which branch campuses may be said to offer 'authentic' American education.[19]

Of all models for international higher education collaboration with China, the branch campus is undoubtedly the most difficult to implement. The British think tank Agora caused much discussion when it published a paper recommending extreme caution for foreign universities when making these sorts of deals. One of the main contributors was the former provost of the University of Nottingham's Ningbo campus, who expressed the view that China perhaps had more to gain through technology and intellectual property transfer than the UK had to gain financially or otherwise from the campus.[20] Whether or not this is a 'true' statement, it does underscore the point that cultural differences become more significant and more difficult to overcome when working with models, such as the branch campus, that require a very high degree of mutual participation and communication. Experts consulted for this project and multiple journalistic sources suggest that universities that attempt to establish branch campuses in China primarily with the profit motive in mind are unlikely to benefit from these ventures. One major problem cited in the Agora report is that in the absence of an overarching national strategy, plans tend to proceed piecemeal and to stray from their original goals.[21]

The Hopkins-Nanjing Center has avoided many of these problems, and has become an internationally recognized institution since it first opened in 1986. Because it is jointly administered by Johns Hopkins University and Nanjing University, some might not consider it a true "branch campus," depending on how this term is defined. In the future, jointly operated institutions may become a separate category of their own. In March 2008, the University of Arizona announced plans to open Nanjing International University with cooperation from Nanjing Normal University and other local partners. The goal is to offer UA-style education to 10,000 students within ten years.[22] If this model proves successful, we may have to start treating jointly administered branch campuses as a separate category of institution, but for the moment there are too few examples of this arrangement.

Hopkins-Nanjing Center

http://nanjing.jhu.edu/index.html

The Hopkins-Nanjing Center offers graduate education in international studies for both Chinese and American students, enrolling equal numbers of each nationality. The Center offers two distinct programs: a two-year Master of Arts in International Studies and a one-year graduate Certificate program. The program is unique in its demanding Chinese language proficiency requirement, and all entering foreigners must receive high marks on the HSK or CAL tests of Chinese language competency. This high language standard allows all courses to be taught in the target language: Mandarin for Americans and English for Chinese students. The Center is also notable for its large, uncensored library, which contains more than 85,000 volumes in English and Chinese.

Missouri State University-Branch Campus, China

http://chinacampus.missouristate.edu

Since June 2000, the Missouri State Branch Campus at Liaoning Normal University has offered a two-year Associate of Arts in General Studies with a business focus, and a two-year completion program that leads to a Bachelor of Science in General Business degree. The Branch Campus programs are fully accredited by the Higher Learning Commission of the North Central Association of Colleges and Schools. The student body is mostly Chinese, but also includes students from Africa, Korea, Indonesia, Mongolia and Hong Kong. Instructors come from the United States, Liaoning Normal University and other countries. Basic knowledge of English is required for admission.

New York Institute of Technology

www.nyit.edu/nyit_worldwide/china/nyit_nupt_nanjing

The New York Institute of Technology opened an American-style undergraduate school in Nanjing, China in fall 2007. The institute is collaborating with the Nanjing University of Posts and Telecommunication (NUPT) to offer English-only education, partially under the teaching of American professors, to 321 Chinese students, with the goal of growing the program to 6,000 students.[23] Students can opt to receive dual degrees from NUPT and NYIT, or just a degree from NYIT, and are eligible to take classes at the New York campus if they can obtain visas. The campus offers majors in computer science, communication arts, and electrical and computer engineering.

Confucius Institutes

Since 2004, when the success of a pilot program in Tashkent, Uzbekistan convinced the Chinese government to expand the model worldwide, China has been establishing Confucius Institutes around the world. These non-profit public institutes aim to promote Chinese language and culture. As of December 2007, there were 210 Confucius Institutes operating in over 60 countries, and approximately 60 Chinese universities and institutes participated in their development and administration.[24] The United States had the greatest number of Confucius Institutes with 39, followed by Thailand, South Korea, and Japan.

Unlike other institutes of this type (British Council, Goethe Institute, Cervantes Institute) many of the Confucius Institutes operate within universities and occasionally high schools. The programs and services offered by Confucius Institutes vary depending on the individual location, but may include introductory courses on Chinese history, geography and culture; Mandarin lessons at various levels including the training of future Mandarin teachers; and resources on China study programs. Confucius Institutes may be found in the United States at the University of Hawaii, Indiana University-Purdue University Indianapolis, the University of Kansas, the University of Oklahoma, the China Institute in New York City, and many other locations throughout the entire country.

Many observers, with varying degrees of praise and caution, have noted that the Confucius Institutes, through their promotion of Chinese culture abroad, serve as vehicles of "soft power" for the Chinese government. One Swedish study summarizes this analysis:

> The undertaking of setting up Confucius Institutes (*Kongzi xueyuan*) abroad … is a practice of employing culture as a medium in managing foreign relations. Its form, the aim that the organization espouses, and the way it operates are revealing; and as a service to China's public diplomacy it constitutes an integral part of China's image management, intended to create and maintain an environment desirable for continued development inside China. The intended audience of this cultural symbol is both domestic and foreign, and the message it delivers is "harmony," a theme chosen by China's current leadership to push for balanced development in the new century. The internal agenda for development has a decisive influence on China's foreign policy.[25]

The Institutes have been overwhelmingly welcomed in the United States, where administrators consider them important to the internationalization of their campuses, as well as to the broader goal of enhancing Sino-American relations. On the occasion of the selection of the University of Oklahoma as the site of a Confucius Institute, President David L. Boren commented:

> It is a great honor for OU to be selected as one of a very small number of universities in the nation to host a Confucius Institute … There is no more important relationship to the security and quality of life for the entire globe during this century than the relationship between China and the United States. OU proudly accepts the challenge to enhance understanding and mutual respect between the people of China and the United States.[26]

Since the Institutes have existed for a very short time, it is too early to say for sure what effect, if any, they will exert on Chinese language and East Asian Studies programs at universities nationwide.

Conclusion

Although these models are diverse and accommodate a broad range of programs, they still refer primarily to U.S. students at the postsecondary level, and as such do not begin to describe the full extent of U.S.-China educational activities. The chapters that follow represent additional aspects of educational cooperation between the two countries. They are intended to provide perspectives on high school exchange, scholar exchange, PRC and U.S. government support, Chinese and American campus coordination, and more. Even these perspectives do not fully describe educational relations between the U.S. and China, but like the models and examples described here, they suggest the diversity of participants and administrators of U.S.-China exchange.

This article was adapted from an unpublished report of the Institute of International Education, "Opportunities and Challenges in U.S.-China Institutional Linkages," which was prepared for the Fund for the Improvement of Postsecondary Education (FIPSE), U.S. Department of Education.

NOTES

[1] Anne F. Thurston and others, *China Bound, Revised: A Guide to Academic Life and Work in the PRC* (Washington, D.C.: National Academy Press, 1994), 239.

[2] Weifang Min, "Historical Perspectives and Contemporary Challenges: The Case of Chinese Universities," Center on Chinese Education, Teacher's College at Columbia University (2006). Available at: www.tc.columbia.edu/centers/coce/pdf_files/c8.pdf.

[3] "Global Destinations for International Students at the Post-Secondary (Tertiary) Level, 2007," *Atlas of Student Mobility*, available online: http://www.atlas.iienetwork.org/?p=48027. *Atlas of Student Mobility* data for China is collected in partnership with the China Scholarship Council and uses the OECD definition of 'international student': "Students are classified as foreign students if they are not citizens of the country for which the data are collected. Countries unable to provide data or estimates for non-nationals on the basis of their passports were requested to substitute data according to a related alternative criterion, e.g., the country of residence, the non-national mother tongue or non-national parentage ... The number of students studying abroad is obtained from the destination countries' reports. Counts of students studying in countries not reporting to the OECD are not included within this indicator."

[4] *Atlas of International Student Mobility*, "Destinations: China, People's Republic (2006)." Available online: http://www.atlas.iienetwork.org/?p=53467.

[5] Rajika Bhandari and Patricia Chow, *Open Doors 2007: Report on International Educational Exchange* (New York: Institute of International Education, 2007); Todd M. Davis, *Open Doors 1996/97: Report on International Educational Exchange* (New York: Institute of International Education, 1997).

[6] *Open Doors* defines international scholars as "… non-immigrant, non-student academics … at U.S. doctoral degree-granting institutions. Scholars may also be affiliated with these institutions for activities such as conferences, colloquia, observations, or consultations."

[7] Nelly Furman and others, "Enrollments in Languages Other than English in United States Institutions of Higher Education, Fall 2006," *Modern Language Association*, 13 November 2007. Available online: http://www.mla.org/pdf/06enrollmentsurvey_final.pdf. Chinese enrollments include Mandarin, and do not include enrollments in Cantonese or Classical Chinese.

[8] Rajika Bhandari and Patricia Chow, *Open Doors 2007: Report on International Educational Exchange* (New York: Institute of International Education, 2007), 69.

[9] We have not restricted program examples solely to programs listed in *IIEPassport*, but we do use *IIEPassport* to discuss trends in study abroad offerings in China. We have used the print directories for this purpose: Marie O'Sullivan, ed., *IIEPassport: Academic Year Abroad, 37th Edition 2008-2009* (New York: Institute of International Education and EducationDynamics, 2007); Marie O'Sullivan, ed., *IIEPassport: Short-Term Study Abroad 58th Edition 2008-2009* (New York: Institute of International Education and EducationDynamics, 2007).

[10] The access date for all program URLs is 6 September, 2008.

[11] Wenying "Nan" Sun and Robert J. Boncella, "Transnational Higher Education: Issues Affecting Joint Degree Programs Among U.S. and Chinese Schools," *Issues in Information Systems* 8, no. 1 (2007): 65.

[12] Sun and Boncella, 67.

[13] Elizabeth Redden, "The Phantom Campus in China," *Inside Higher Ed*, 12 February 2008.

[14] "The Case for Engagement: An Interview with Richard Levin," *The Politic*, 6 September 2007. Available Online: http://thepolitic.org/content/view/53/37.

[15] Li Han, "Tsinghua-Johns Hopkins Joint Center for Biomedical Engineering Opens," *Tsinghua University News*, 8 January 2008. Available online: http://news.tsinghua.edu.cn/eng__news.php?id=1511.

[16] These are the only two American branch campuses in China identified by the *Open Doors 2007* branch campuses survey. See the following for more information: http://opendoors.iienetwork.org/?p=branchcampuses.

[17] Redden.

[18] Netherlands Education Support Office Beijing, 24.

[19] "U.S. Universities Rush to Set Up Outposts Abroad," *New York Times*, 10 February 2008. Available online: http://www.nytimes.com/2008/02/10/education/10global.html.

[20] Paul Mooney, "British Universities Should be More Cautious in Collaborating With China", *The Chronicle*, 7 December 2007.

[21] Anna Fazackerly, ed. "British Universities in China: The Reality Beyond the Rhetoric. An Agora Discussion Paper." (December 2007), 1. Available online: www.agora-education.org.

[22] "University of Arizona to Provide Academic Content for New Chinese School," *The Business Journal of Phoenix*, 4 March 2008. Available online: www.bizjournals.com/phoenix/stories/2008/03/03/daily23.html.

[23] "New York Institute of Technology Opens American-Style University in China," *NYIT News,* 17 October 2007. Available online: www.nyit.edu/news/current/article_220/article.html.

[24] Xiaolin Guo, "Repackaging Confucius: PRC Diplomacy and the Rise of Soft Power" (Stockholm-Nacka, Sweden: Institute for Security and Development Policy, 2008), 31.

[25] Ibid., 9.

[26] "Confucius Institute to be Established at OU," *OU Public Affairs*, 16 August 2006. Available online: http://casweb.ou.edu/home/news/press/press_20060816.html.

Chapter Two

NATIONAL POLICY GOALS: U.S. GOVERNMENT ACTIVITIES SUPPORTING U.S.-CHINA EXCHANGE

BY THOMAS A. FARRELL, DEPUTY ASSISTANT SECRETARY FOR ACADEMIC PROGRAMS, U.S. DEPARTMENT OF STATE, BUREAU OF EDUCATIONAL AND CULTURAL AFFAIRS

Introduction

As China's influence in the world grows, the need to increase understanding between the people of the U.S. and the people of China grows as well. International educational exchanges play a key role in the bilateral U.S.-China relationship, providing the context and underpinning for dialogue and negotiation on a wide range of economic, political and social issues. U.S. government resources and attention to exchanges with the People's Republic of China—which now has one of the largest Fulbright Programs in the world—demonstrate the value that we place on these exchanges.

While understanding is not always synonymous with agreement, increased knowledge reduces stereotypes and corrects mistaken assumptions, promoting decision-making based on accurate perceptions about the other country and its people. As the U.S. negotiates the complex issues of the twenty-first century, having more leaders in China in a wide range of fields who have studied here, and more Americans in leadership positions who speak Chinese and have direct knowledge of the country and its institutions, will be crucial to successfully addressing issues in our relationship and developing solutions to shared problems.

The U.S. government plays a leading role in educational exchanges with China, both responding to Chinese interests and championing those areas of study and research that represent the highest achievements of American society. While a number of U.S. federal agencies support exchanges with China, the Department of State has the lead authority in negotiating formal exchange agreements and conducting international educational and exchange activities with other countries around the world, including China.

Our efforts with China include the area of language acquisition of both English and Mandarin, a foundation for international academic study and exchanges, where the U.S. seeks to strengthen the comprehensive language learning pipeline in both nations. In the broader field of leadership development, the State Department seeks to ensure that individual exchange participants gain an increased understanding of the other society that they can draw upon and share with their colleagues and institutions after they return home, and as they reach positions of greater influence in education, government, business, the sciences, the arts and other fields.

China is included in virtually all the educational exchange programs administered by the Bureau of Educational and Cultural Affairs (ECA) of the Department of State. In 2006, the ECA Bureau, which funds and administers the worldwide Fulbright Program through its annual appropriation from the U.S. Congress, provided a major increase in financial support for Fulbright academic exchanges with China, as did the Government of China, under a new joint Fulbright agreement.

State's ECA Bureau also brings Chinese mid-career professionals to the U.S. for a year of academic study and professional experience under the Humphrey Fellowship Program for countries in development and transition; sends American undergraduates who are Pell Grant recipients to study abroad in China and learn Chinese under the worldwide Gilman Program; supports two-way professional development exchanges for Chinese and U.S. teachers; and brings Chinese undergraduates to the U.S. for intensive study and leadership development programs on U.S. campuses.

Chinese is one of seven languages and language families in the Presidential National Security Language Initiative (NSLI), an effort of four federal agencies launched in 2006 and coordinated by the White House to increase Americans' knowledge and mastery of critical languages. The State Department supports language-related exchanges of high school, undergraduate and graduate level students and teachers under NSLI.

The creation of a new State Department Regional English Language Officer position in China in 2007 greatly enhanced U.S. Government-sponsored English teaching efforts there.

The ECA Bureau's educational programs emphasize individual academic and leadership development, providing scholarships and exchange opportunities to U.S. students, scholars, teachers and professionals for study, teaching and research overseas, and to individuals from other countries to participate in educational exchanges and programs with the U.S. Programs are designed with merit-based selection processes, with the goal of meeting bilateral priorities, and promoting access and inclusion. Sustaining interaction with and among the alumni of these programs is increasingly a priority for the Bureau as well. Virtually all these exchanges are administered in partnership with U.S. non-governmental organizations, through cooperative agreements awarded through the Bureau's Congressionally mandated competitive grants process.

Evaluation of impact and effectiveness is an increasingly important element of the exchanges administered by the Bureau. Recent assessments by the Office of Management and Budget have given the ECA Bureau one of the highest ratings in the federal government for its evaluation efforts. State's ECA Bureau officers are closely involved in the administration of these exchanges, in cooperation with U.S. NGO partner organizations, and seek continuous improvements in their quality, efficiency and effectiveness.

China is currently one of the top sending countries of foreign students to the U.S. for university study worldwide. The State Department supports educational advising about U.S. higher education in China, supported a joint delegation of U.S. college and university presidents and senior U.S. government officials to China to promote U.S. higher education, and co-sponsored, with the U.S. Department of Commerce, the creation of a video to market U.S. higher education to Chinese audiences.

While State Department-sponsored educational exchanges, such as the flagship Fulbright Program, play an important role in the bilateral relationship, the majority of educational exchanges with China still take place under non-governmental U.S. auspices, reflecting the decentralization and open and diverse nature of the U.S. educational system and society. The State Department values and encourages these direct exchanges by U.S. and Chinese institutions and counterparts, which supplement, enhance and complement our government-supported exchanges. At the same time, the government-sponsored exchanges often serve as catalysts and can help to shape and support the role of all exchanges, both public and private, in serving the national interest.

Fulbright Program

The first Fulbright Program anywhere in the world was with China. The program was established by formal agreement between the two governments in 1947, when the first Fulbright accord was signed by Chinese Foreign Minister Wang Shiqie and American Ambassador J. Leighton Stuart. By August 1949, 27 American scholars and students and 24 Chinese students and scholars had taken part in the program, but it ceased operation that same year, when the People's Republic of China was founded and diplomatic relations between the two countries were temporarily suspended. The U.S.-China Fulbright Program was not reestablished until thirty years later, in 1979. Today, the Fulbright Program with China is one of the largest in the world, an expression of the importance that both nations attach to the government-supported exchange of students, teachers and scholars to promote mutual understanding.

Fulbright is a worldwide program that was created in the immediate aftermath of the Second World War, when the late Senator J. William Fulbright of Arkansas introduced legislation authorizing a program of educational and cultural exchange. The legislation, signed by President Truman, amended the Surplus Property Act of 1944, making it possible to use foreign credits from the sale of U.S. surplus war properties abroad to fund the program. Viewed historically, the Fulbright Program can be seen as one of a number of new institutions that were created following the end of the War, institutions that constituted a new international architecture. The Fulbright Program, the Bretton Woods system of international economic cooperation, the United Nations, the World Bank, the International Monetary Fund, and the Marshall Plan were all a reflection of the view that new international institutions were needed to serve a new post-War world.

In the early 1980s, after the Fulbright Program with China was resumed, each country seemed to view the program somewhat differently. China saw the program principally, although not exclusively, as a means of enhancing its modernization efforts and as a vehicle that would enable its future leaders to acquire technological and scientific expertise. The U.S. sought to emphasize U.S. studies, encompassing such disciplines as history, literature, law, economics, politics, and international relations, to promote greater understanding of the nature of U.S. society. The U.S. Fulbright scholar/lecturer program focused on the teaching of English, American literature, and history at four institutions in Beijing, Tianjin and Shanghai. Over the ensuing years, the Fulbright Program in China has continued to expand, both in terms of fields of lectureships and in the number of Chinese universities hosting Fulbright Scholars. Nearly fifty institutions throughout the country were participating in the program by 2008, most of them universities under the direct jurisdiction of the Ministry of Education.

As of 2008, about 165 participants are funded each year under the Fulbright Program with China. The core program includes four major components:

1. The **U.S. Student Program,** which sends about 70 American students to China annually;

2. The **U.S. Scholar Program**, which sends approximately 20 lecturers and 15 researchers to China each year;

3. The **China Student Program** that brings 20 Ph.D. candidates to the U.S. for a year of dissertation-related research; and

4. The **China Researchers Program**, which brings about 40 Chinese scholars each year to the U.S.

These programs are managed by the Bureau of Educational and Cultural Affairs in Washington and by the U.S. Embassy in Beijing. In the U.S., the Bureau is assisted by the Institute of International Education in New York, and its affiliate, the Council for International Exchange of Scholars in Washington, D.C., in administering the student and scholar application, peer review and nomination processes.

In China, students and scholars apply for awards through their universities and under the auspices of the China Scholarship Council, an organization that works closely with the Chinese Ministry of Education. Panels of Chinese and U.S. government representatives review applications and nominate slates of candidates, who, once approved, are placed by CIES and IIE at U.S. academic institutions. The IIE Beijing office also works with the U.S. Embassy in Beijing, providing services to both Chinese Fulbright students and scholars bound for the United States, and U.S. Fulbright students and scholars who travel to China each year. Applicants for the relatively new Chinese Fulbright student program must be enrolled in doctoral programs in China. The program for Chinese scholars supports research at U.S. universities by Chinese scholars in a wide range of disciplines.

Under the National Security Language Initiative, the State Department has dramatically expanded the **Fulbright Foreign Language Teaching Assistants Program (FLTA)** with China. The program currently brings about 40 young Chinese teachers to the U.S. annually as teaching assistants of Mandarin at U.S. colleges and universities. The teachers, who in China are professional teachers of English, serve as teaching assistants in college and university classrooms for a year, while also taking courses in English language pedagogy and U.S. studies fields, increasing their knowledge and skills as teachers of English when they return to China.

U.S. students apply to the Institute of International Education for Fulbright scholarships following a U.S. campus application process. Recent college graduates through advanced graduate students are eligible to apply, but all applicants must have studied Mandarin for at least two years, to promote the achievement of the applicant's academic project in China. U.S. Fulbright students apply in a range of disciplines; the study of Chinese society and culture is a central element of most research projects, which are in the humanities and social sciences, including literature, environmental studies, history, music, economics, and other fields. IIE convenes faculty panels to review applications and make recommendations to the Fulbright Foreign Scholarship Board, an independent, Presidentially appointed board of distinguished private citizens, which is responsible for the final selection of all Fulbright awardees.

U.S. students selected for the Fulbright Program with China may apply to participate in intensive Mandarin study in China prior to taking up their Fulbright grants, under NSLI. Currently, approximately one third of the annual cohort of U.S. Fulbright students to China receives a language study enhancement award.

U.S. Fulbright scholars (postdoctoral/terminal degree) may apply for lecturing or research awards through the Council for International Exchange of Scholars, which annually convenes peer review panels that recommend candidates for awards. The peer review process is a central element of the Fulbright Program, serving as a guarantor of the program's scholarly integrity, and non-partisan and non-political character.

Most U.S. applicants for research scholar awards at the scholar level are Sinologists; U.S. lecturers usually teach in humanities or social sciences fields, with a particular emphasis on law in recent years. The lecturers are placed at universities throughout China, for a semester or full academic year.

U.S. support for the Fulbright program is predicated on the assumption that free and open inquiry is both a reflection of core American values, and critical to increasing understanding between the people of the United States and China.

English Language Programs

English Language Programs have gained importance among the ECA Bureau's programs with China and other countries, reflecting growing awareness of the role of English in opening doors to educational and economic opportunity as well as to study in the U.S. Around the world, English study is in high demand by governments as well as students and their families. Providing English training to talented Chinese students from disadvantaged sectors, who would not otherwise have the opportunity to learn English well, removes a critical barrier that allows them to compete to take part in exchanges and study in the United States, helping to make exchanges more fully representative of Chinese society.

The ECA Bureau supports English language programs in a variety of ways. A **Regional English Language Officer (RELO)** who belongs to State's corps of foreign service officers with specialized expertise in the teaching of English, is based at the U.S. Embassy in Beijing. This officer coordinates the Bureau's English teaching programs on the Chinese mainland and in Hong Kong.

The **English Language Fellow Program** sends highly qualified U.S. educators in the field of teaching English to speakers of other languages on ten-month fellowships to academic institutions in China. Fellows work with local faculty at the university level to build English language teaching capacity. The **English Language Specialist Program** sends U.S. educators and scholars in English teaching and applied linguistics on two- to four-week assignments abroad. Specialists work on specific assignments at the request of U.S. embassies.

Established in 2004 as a program for countries in the Middle East and South Asia, the **English Access Microscholarship Program** has expanded to over 50 countries, including China. The program provides a foundation of English language skills to talented 14-to 18-year-olds from disadvantaged sectors through after-school classes and intensive summer learning activities. About 60 Chinese students were selected to receive English Access Microscholarships in 2007-2008.

The **E-Teacher Scholarship Program** seeks to improve the quality of overseas English language teaching through the use innovative distance learning technology. Participants are English teaching professionals who receive instruction from U.S. experts in current English language teaching methods and techniques. Courses in the E-Teacher Scholarship Program include Assessment, English for Business, English for Law, Teaching Critical Thinking, and Teaching English to Young Learners.

The Office of English Language Programs also produces the *English Teaching Forum*, a quarterly journal for overseas teachers of English that focuses on methods and practices.

Hubert H. Humphrey Program

The **Hubert H. Humphrey Fellowship Program**, a component of the Fulbright Program, brings mid-career professionals from countries in development and transition to the U.S. for a year of non-degree, graduate-level work and professional development. There were five Humphrey Fellows from China in the 2007-2008 academic year and seven new Fellows were selected for the 2008-2009 academic year. There are 91 Chinese Humphrey Fellow alumni. The program is managed by the Public Affairs Section of the U.S. Embassy, in cooperation with the Bureau of Educational and Cultural Affairs, and the U.S. non-governmental partner, the Institute of International Education.

The Benjamin A. Gilman International Scholarship Program

The **Benjamin A. Gilman International Scholarship Program** supports study abroad by American undergraduate students with financial need. The program emphasizes inclusion of students from diverse backgrounds and students going to non-traditional study abroad destinations. More than 200 Gilman students have studied in China since the program's inception in 2001. The Gilman Program also provides supplements for Chinese language study to selected U.S. students during their award, as a component of the National Security Language Initiative. Currently, the Bureau supports about 80 students annually for study in China, representing approximately 13 percent of annual Gilman awardees.

Chinese Language Study

In addition to Chinese language study and teaching awards provided through the Gilman and U.S. Fulbright student programs, and the Fulbright Foreign Language Teaching Assistant Program, the ECA Bureau supports a large program of **Intensive Summer Language Institutes** for U.S. undergraduate and graduate students to study critical languages abroad. Approximately 80 awards are offered for summer language study in China by U.S. university-level students. In addition, about 80 U.S. high school students will embark upon six-week programs of intensive study in Beijing and Shanghai.

Under the ECA Bureau's **Teacher Exchange Program**, Chinese educators teach Mandarin in U.S. classrooms for an academic year. Over the past two years, 21 U.S. teachers have received fellowships to improve their Mandarin language skills and cultural knowledge through intensive summer study in China; and 23 Chinese teachers have received awards to teach Mandarin in U.S. elementary and secondary schools across the country, while participating in professional development and cultural enrichment activities. China also participates in other two-way professional development teacher exchanges sponsored by the ECA Bureau.

Student Advising

The ECA Bureau supports 45 educational advising centers in China by providing educational reference material and professional development training for advisers to enable the centers to provide accurate and complete information to Chinese students and their families about study opportunities in the U.S. Centers are located in different institutions, including the U.S. Embassy and its branch public affairs offices in China; the Chinese Service Center for Scholarly Exchange; selected universities; and libraries. An educational advising country coordinator, based at the American Center in Beijing, facilitates the participation of Chinese educational advisers in professional development opportunities and advises U.S. university representatives about recruitment of Chinese students to study in the U.S. and in identifying study options in China for U.S. students. The coordinator also organizes pre-departure and general orientation sessions for Chinese students, maintains a Chinese language website, and provides virtual consulting services.

The Institute of International Education's *Open Doors* annual survey on international educational exchange, which is funded by State's ECA Bureau, reported that 67,723 Chinese students were enrolled in U.S. institutions of higher education in 2006-07, the most recent year for which confirmed data are available. This number represents an 8.2 percent increase over the previous year. China is the second largest source of international students for U.S. higher education (after India). Of the total number of Chinese students who are in the U.S., 14.7 percent studied at the undergraduate level and 70.8 percent enrolled in graduate programs, with the remainder having participated in short-term training programs. On the U.S. side of student exchanges, *Open Doors* reports that 8,830 U.S. students studied in China in non-degree programs in 2005/06 for credit received back at their home institutions, which represented an increase of 38.2 percent from the previous year.

Conclusion

Educational exchange programs, while benefiting individuals by increasing their knowledge and enabling them to build personal and professional relationships in the country of their exchange, also serve a larger set of interests, by strengthening mutual understanding between peoples and among nations. The evidence of the effectiveness of these programs are its many alumni, who can be found today in positions of leadership throughout the institutions of both societies, thereby building a foundation of trust between the leaders and citizens of the United States and of China.

Background on ECA

The Department of State is the Executive Branch Department authorized by the Congress of the United States to conduct official U.S. public diplomacy programs abroad, including educational exchanges. Exchange programs reflect the long-term foreign policy interests of the U.S. in promoting increased understanding and constructive interaction between individuals, institutions and publics in the United States and other countries. The State Department's ECA Bureau supports a wide range of educational, professional and cultural exchanges involving educators, students, scientists, artists, government officials, journalists, NGO representatives and members of the business community, among others. Central to these exchanges is the goal of advancing mutual understanding between the people of the United States and the people of other countries, as embodied in the Fulbright-Hays legislation (Mutual Educational and Cultural Affairs Exchange Act of 1961.) The ECA Bureau supports academic exchanges on a bilateral basis, through the Public Affairs Sections of U.S. embassies and binational Fulbright Commissions, in cooperation with partner governments in more than 150 countries.

Chapter Three

NATIONAL POLICY GOALS: PRC GOVERNMENT ACTIVITIES SUPPORTING U.S.-CHINA EXCHANGE

BY YANG XINYU, DEPUTY SECRETARY-GENERAL, CHINA SCHOLARSHIP COUNCIL

Since the adoption of China's Open Door Policy thirty years ago, educational exchange has grown tremendously from limited student exchange to many forms of exchange, including student/faculty exchange, research collaboration, joint and dual degree programs, jointly operated schools and programs, and joint academic conferences. On December 26, 1978, the arrival of 52 Chinese visiting scholars to New York's JFK Airport marked the first Chinese government-sponsored study abroad program since the Cultural Revolution. This was the first group of scholars supported by the Chinese government to study in the United States since 1941. To make this happen, the two governments made enormous efforts and provided great support even though there were no formal diplomatic relations between the two countries at the time. Since then, more and more higher education institutions all around the world have opened their doors to Chinese students, and China now sends the largest number of students abroad for international education. With the development of higher education in China and increasing recognition of the quality of Chinese higher education by the international community, China has also gradually become one of the most popular destination countries for international education. In 2007, 144,000 Chinese students left China to study abroad, and this brought the total number of Chinese students currently studying overseas to 657,200. Meanwhile, 195,503 international students studied in 544 Chinese higher education institutions in the year 2007 according to the China Scholarship Council.

China's social and economic development have benefited greatly from the Open Door policy in the past 30 years. Support from both the Chinese and U.S. governments has produced fruitful results and promoted the fast development of higher education and scientific research in China.

The Development and Challenges of Higher Education in China

The last thirty years and especially the last ten years have seen great developments in Chinese higher education. In 1999, the central government made a major decision to expand the recruitment of higher education institutions. Since then, many more young Chinese students have had the opportunity to receive higher education. At the same time, the structure of some higher education institutions was rearranged, resulting in the merging of formerly separate institutions. These mergers made the universities more comprehensive by international standards and also greatly increased their size. Today, the largest university in China is Jilin University in Changchun City, with full-time enrollment of nearly 70,000 students. The rapid increase in enrollment created a number of serious problems, including quality control and efficient financing. Today, the Chinese government and Chinese higher education institutions face the challenge of how to help the higher education system fulfill its obligation to cultivate talent and serve the social and economic development of the country.

The Development of Higher Education in China

By 2007, total higher education enrollment was 18 million, compared with 6.8 million in 1998. The enrollment rate reached 15% by 2002, compared to 9.8% in 1998, as higher education began to enroll not just the elite, but also the masses. This rate further increased to 23% in 2007. The expansion of higher education has made a major contribution to China's rapid development.

The Chinese government implemented two major projects for the development of Chinese higher education institutions, Project 211 and Project 985. Project 211 concentrates on the development of 100 Chinese universities in the 21st century. The main focus is to readjust the structure of the disciplines and upgrade the quality of teaching and research. Project 985 was initiated in May 1998 with the goal of elevating a small number of Chinese universities to world-class status and international recognition. The universities involved in these two projects enjoyed favorable policies and received special funding for facility improvement, professional development and attracting leading scientists. The overall quality and competitiveness of universities improved greatly as a result. In the last ten years, the research funding of these universities and the academic papers included in the Science Citation Index both have seen a seven-fold increase.

Traditionally, scientific research in China was done mainly by the research institutes of the Chinese Academy of Sciences and the Chinese Academy of Social Sciences, but as China has developed in the past decades, universities have gradually become a major force for scientific research. From 2002-2007, 90 National Natural Science Awards (58%), 89 National Awards for Technological Invention (64%), and 543 National Awards of Scientific Progress (55%) went to university faculty. In 2006, the three major national science awards all recognized university faculty. Forty percent of the fellows of Chinese Academy of Sciences and Chinese Academy of Engineering are university professors. Universities in China have gradually become a major research base, and are increasingly competing successfully for national-level research funds.

The quality of higher education in China has improved dramatically, and countries around the world are beginning to recognize this. By 2007, 32 countries had signed agreements with the Chinese Ministry of Education on mutual recognition of academic degrees. These countries include the United Kingdom, France, Germany, Australia, New Zealand and many others. In many countries, universities welcome Chinese students for graduate study because of their good reputation for diligence and solid knowledge foundation.

The continuous increase of funding from the government and other sources has enabled the rapid development of higher education in China. Although higher education funding increased at an annual rate of 24.5% from 1998-2005, even this rapid increase is not quite sufficient. From 1998-2006, the total size of all university campuses enlarged by 260%, total classroom space increased by 370%, and the total value of research facilities increased by 470%, all of which contributed to a great improvement in teaching and research conditions.

In 1998, the Ministry of Education established a student aid system. Four million students benefit from these national scholarship and loan programs every year. The Ministry of Education's goal is to make higher education affordable for all qualified students.

The Challenges of Higher Education in China

Although visible achievements have been made, Chinese higher education faces critical challenges, especially after the sudden increase in student enrollment over a very short time. The overall level of higher education is still far behind that of the world's prestigious universities.

First, there is the problem of unbalanced development in different regions in China. The overall structure and distribution and the curriculum design cannot really meet the needs of social and economic development in under-developed regions. Students from different regions do not enjoy equivalent access to higher education opportunities.

Secondly, the traditional patterns of talent cultivation, teaching methodology and course content are not sufficient to educate students in innovation or practical skills. The lack of highly qualified teaching and research staff seriously affect the quality of education. Without leading scientists in many fields, the quality of research is also facing great challenges.

Thirdly, although there have been enormous increases in higher education financing over the past ten years, they have not been able to keep up with the fast pace of development. Some universities that seek to meet their budget needs through bank loans may be burdened by difficulties in repaying these loans.

Finally, Chinese universities are facing growing pressure due to the rising unemployment rate among graduates. University graduates are no longer guaranteed jobs upon graduation, as they were twenty years ago. The universities should consider making changes to the teaching process to better meet the requirements of the fast growing market economy.

China's development has unique characteristics, and it can be difficult to adapt the experiences of others to this context. By opening their doors to the outside world, Chinese higher education institutions could discuss these problems with partners from other countries, see their own problems from a broader standpoint, and make changes based on what they have learned through this exchange.

Study Abroad and its Impact on China's Social and Economic Development

Thirty years ago, when China adopted the Open Door Policy, the first step at the outset was to send Chinese students and scholars to study abroad. From 1978-2007, 1.2 million study fellows pursued further study overseas. Among them, 320,000 returned, and 657,200 are currently studying or carrying out research in higher education institutions all around the world. The returned study fellows play a very important role in China's higher education system, as well as social and economic development.

Scale, Level and Priority

The number of Chinese students headed abroad for study has increased very rapidly in the last ten years from tens of thousands in 1998 to 144,000 in 2007. About 5-10% of them were sponsored by government or home institutions. The rest are sponsored either by family or host institutions; these students are considered self-sponsored students. There are great differences in trends among government-sponsored versus self-sponsored students in the level of study, field of study and placement. Government-sponsored study abroad programs mandate very clear priorities for level and field of study. They mainly support graduate study and postdoctoral research or research collaboration. The priority fields of study include IT and telecommunications, energy and environment, life science and public health, engineering, agriculture, material science and applied social sciences. The purpose of these programs is to train outstanding young graduate students and upgrade the level of university faculty, research staff and government officials by putting them in an international learning environment. Self-financed students have a more diverse set of motivations for studying abroad, and the majority of overseas Chinese students are abroad for undergraduate study. The overseas study experience is surely beneficial to one's personal development.

Policy

Study abroad activities in China are greatly supported by Chinese government policy. In the early eighties, only government-sponsored study fellows had the opportunity to study abroad. The focus at that time was to send as many highly qualified candidates abroad as possible, because after the Cultural Revolution, China desperately needed large numbers of well-trained, talented graduates for its development. Without government sponsorship, at that time no one would have dreamed of pursuing overseas studies as an individual or personal matter. Only students who had close relatives living overseas to support them financially were allowed to study abroad independent of government sponsorship. The policy changed in 1986 to allow self-financed students and scholars to study abroad. This new policy encouraged them to return to China on completion of study abroad. Chinese citizens could apply for approval to pursue self-financed study abroad from their home institution, but had to pay back to the home institution an amount equivalent to government expenditure per student. At this time, the cost of higher education in China was covered entirely by the government.

The establishment of the China Scholarship Council was a milestone in study abroad policy development. As a result of the rearrangement of central government departments, CSC was set up by the Ministry of Education and charged with administering government scholarship programs. The selection of scholarship recipients represented a major change from assigned allocations to open competition.

The Chinese government also set up a number of favorable policies to encourage students to return to China after their studies. By the late 1980s, the government was facing public pressure because many government-sponsored study fellows, for various reasons, were not returning to China immediately after the completion of their studies. This was not an isolated issue. It was more complicated than the choice not to return, it was an issue of policy, environment, and living and working conditions. The situation became even worse after the June 4th Tiananmen Square event. Some countries extended special immigration policies to Chinese students, and some even provided them political protection. It was a difficult time for the Chinese government, and for Chinese institutions worried about losing their staff or students.

It was Deng Xiaoping, once again, who offered comments on how to deal with this issue. When he traveled to Shenzhen, China's first special economic zone, he stated that the Chinese government should think about making special policies to encourage overseas study fellows to return. He suggested that the government and home institutions should provide good working and living conditions and necessary funds to help them settle down, regardless of their political attitudes. He then passed on the message to overseas Chinese students, telling them that it was better to return if they wished to contribute to the social and economic development of China.

Following these developments, the Chinese government issued a number of official documents clearly indicating preferential policies on salary, health care, welfare, working conditions, employment of spouses, etc. The Ministry of Education also set up projects especially for overseas Chinese study fellows, including the "Research Fund of Returned Study Fellows," the "Cheung Kong Scholars Project," and the "Chunhui Project." The Natural Science Foundation of China also set up special programs to attract overseas Chinese students, the most important of which is the "National Research Fund for Outstanding Young Scientists." Winners of this project are eligible for funds sufficient to conduct research either in natural science or applied basic research. Another example is the "One Hundred Talents Project" of the Chinese Academy of Sciences, which aims to attract back 100 talented overseas Chinese students annually to be leading scientists in research institutes. Provincial and local governments also made efforts to welcome study fellows to start businesses or bring investments to their regions. Local governments have established over twenty science parks for returned study fellows throughout China to serve as incubators for the returned study fellows to start businesses.

In recent years, "The Mid to Long Term Strategy of Scientific Research," a national project for the strategic development of science and technology, and the launch of Project 211 and Project 985 have provided great opportunities to those who remained overseas to return and join in the exciting process of social and economic development.

With the growing tendency of talented researchers to compete on a global scale, the Chinese government, like many others, is making more efforts to attract top scientists from all around the world to be leaders of major national projects.

Scholarships

China is among the few countries that provide large numbers of scholarships to support international education for their own citizens as well as international students. When the late Chinese leader Deng Xiaoping initiated support for young Chinese students to study abroad in 1978, the Chinese government set up a special budget to provide 3,000 scholarships each year for study abroad. The number of outgoing scholarships has expanded dramatically in recent years to 12,000 annually. The scholarships for international students to study in China have also expanded, and currently the government provides over 10,000 scholarships each year. By 2010, the Chinese government will offer 20,000 scholarships to international students in China annually.

In the late 1970s and early 1980s, Chinese government scholarship holders for study abroad were mainly university faculty or researchers from the Chinese Academy of Sciences and the Chinese Academy of Social Sciences. They were selected by their home institutions and approved by the Ministry of Education, which administered all government scholarship programs. The first ever group of scholars sent by the government after 1978 went to the United States under an oral agreement between the two governments. After that, the governments of the United Kingdom, Germany, France, Japan, Canada, and Australia reached similar agreements with Chinese government on student exchange. Since there were very few contacts between Chinese universities and universities in other countries, governments had to work carefully to place Chinese students in foreign universities. There were no TOFEL or GRE or IELTS examinations in China in those days. Foreign universities found that it was difficult to judge the quality of Chinese students who wished to pursue graduate study because they had no idea of Chinese students' academic background and language level. To solve this problem, the American-Chinese Nobel Laureate Dr. Tsung-Dao Lee initiated a program named "China-U.S. Physics Examination and Application (CUS-PEA)," with the support of the Chinese government. For this program, a number of U.S. universities set up a special test in English at the same standard as they set to accept international students. Chinese students who passed the test were accepted by U.S. universities for PhD study. From 1989-1999 over 900 Chinese students attended

PhD programs at more than 50 U.S. universities under CUSPEA. The contribution of the program was that U.S. universities recognized the quality of Chinese students.

Today, government scholarship holders make up only a very small proportion of all study abroad students, compared to the large number students who are self-sponsored or sponsored by the host university. But because of the opportunities originally provided by government scholarships, a channel was established and the lucky scholars and students who studied abroad in the early 1980s brought back the message that study abroad was possible and that Chinese students had a good chance of being admitted by foreign universities.

After CSC was established, many tailor-made scholarship programs were designed in line with the development of Chinese higher education institutions and China's social and economic development. For example, the "University Young Faculty Training Program" was designed to support development of young faculty members at Chinese universities through study abroad. The "Special Professional Development Program for Western China" was designed to support the national goal of development in western China by funding study abroad fellows from universities and research institutes in that region.

On January 8, 2007, the Chinese government launched a new "Graduate Study Abroad Scholarship Program" which provides 5,000 scholarships every year to university students for graduate study overseas. The main objective of the program is to contribute to the development of Chinese universities and to support the national project of building world-class universities. A select number of Chinese universities are invited to participate in this program. The participating universities have the obligation to select the best students and send them to the best programs under the best possible supervision. Ideally, the program envisions that when students return on completion of their study overseas, they could become university faculty members. The ideal model is that through sending students abroad, the Chinese universities can strengthen academic links with their international partners, and cooperation between Chinese and foreign universities will thus be more efficient.

China is the number one place of origin for students seeking transnational education, and many self-sponsored Chinese students can be found in countries worldwide. To honor their academic achievements, the Chinese government set up the "Award to Outstanding Self-financed Chinese Study Abroad Students" in 2003. Three hundred PhD students receive the award each year based on their study and research performance. The objective of the program is to show that the government sends its care and good wishes to self-financed students, even though it does not sponsor them.

The Impact of Study Abroad

In the past thirty years, 320,000 study fellows have returned to China after completing their studies overseas. Many of them have become leaders in their fields. Statistics show that 78% of Chinese key university presidents, 95% of the directors of CAS research institutes, 60% of the directors of the institutes of CASS, 81% of the fellows of Chinese Academy of Sciences and Chinese Academy of Engineering, 72% of the directors of National Key Laboratories, 94% of Cheung Kong Scholars, and 72% of the chief scientists of the National 973 Project (National Strategic Project of Scientific Research") have studied overseas. Their continuous contribution to China's social and economic development is highly valued.

In 2002, the Higher Education Institution of Peking University conducted a research project on the efficiency of government-sponsored study abroad programs since 1978. The research studied and analyzed the costs and returns of government policy in support of study abroad. The research findings indicated that international education has made great contributions to the reform and development of higher education in China. The returned study fellows are a major force in raising the level of teaching and research at higher education institutions. The value and influence of international education in this process cannot be overstated. The main gains from study abroad according to this research are as follows:

Individual gains:

1. Broadened vision and changed mentality:

   All the returned study fellows who responded to the Peking University questionnaire feel that the most important gain is broadened vision and changed mentality. Many of them experienced "culture shock" when they first arrived and lived in a different culture and environment. While studying and working in foreign universities and research institutes, the Chinese study fellows gained first-hand experience of foreign academic cultures by participating in teaching and research activities. They were greatly influenced by the ideas, teaching methodology, and scientific research mentality that they encountered abroad. These experiences caused the study fellows to consider the gap between China and the western world in quality of teaching and research from a much wider perspective.

2. Upgraded knowledge and enhanced capability:

   Most of study fellows were placed in laboratories or departments that had a very good reputation in their fields. They received guidance from their host professors and worked with them jointly on research. Visible results of their experience include improving their foreign language level, gaining the ability to conduct research, identifying research interests, better understanding the requirements and academic culture of the international community of scientific research, having access to the most advance research material and information, learning the method of managing research projects, and establishing close academic links with their counterparts all around the world.

3. Academic promotion:

   Having experienced study abroad can be beneficial to returned study fellows as they seek academic promotion. Many universities in China have academic policies specifying that along with academic achievements, overseas study or research experience also counts toward academic promotion. They believe that without such experience, it is hard to imagine a scholar possessing international vision and being competitive internationally.

The individual gains of the returned study fellows are not purely "personal," but also include social benefits.

Social benefits:

1. Fostering a new generation of academics with international perspective and the ability to communicate with their international counterparts;

2. Building the backbone of university and research institute leadership and administration, including presidents, vice-presidents, and international office directors;

3. Upgrading knowledge in all fields;

4. Developing new curricula and teaching materials;

5. Introducing advanced teaching methodology;

6. Upgrading and standardizing the level of scientific research;

7. Establishing international networks for educational and research collaboration;

8. Promoting better understanding between China and the western world.

Although many Chinese students and scholars have remained overseas, they play a unique role in cooperation between China and the rest of the world in many fields. With China much more open than in the past, scholars and students who remain overseas are encouraged to contribute to China's social and economic development in many ways.

Chinese Government Activities Supporting U.S.-China Exchange

In Washington, DC on April 2, 2008, the first ever "U.S.-China Education Consultation" was held between the U.S. Department of Education and the Chinese Ministry of Education, with the U.S. Department of State also participating. This was the first ministerial level dialogue on several issues of interest to both governments. The topics discussed included math education, language learning, student and teacher exchanges in language fields, student and scholar exchanges in higher education, and research collaboration. The topics discussed show that the two sides are interested in many forms of collaboration, from primary school math teaching to high level research partnerships. This is a great difference from when the two countries began educational cooperation thirty years ago with only a few exchange students and mostly one-way student flows from China to the U.S.

On August 15, 2008, 150 students from universities in Sichuan Province arrived at New York's JFK Airport. These students came to the United States through a program initiated by the State University of New York to provide opportunities and scholarships to university students from Sichuan Province who are originally from regions of China affected by the May 12, 2008 earthquake. The program allows them to study at SUNY campuses for one academic year. SUNY made great efforts to show sympathy and good wishes to Sichuan Province and wanted to offer help in a special way. The university also passed on the message that people from other parts of the world were concerned and willing to help with the reconstruction of the region. National leaders of China, Sichuan Provincial Government officials, and universities in Sichuan all highly appreciated this gesture. The U.S. Department of State provided great support to facilitate processing travel documents for the students. The China Scholarship Council has offered return tickets for all 150 students.

Through the joint efforts of the Ministry of Education, China Scholarship Council, the U.S. Embassy in Beijing, the U.S. Consulate General in Chengdu, the Sichuan Provincial Education Bureau, the 13 participating universities in Sichuan Province, SUNY, and all the candidates, all 150 students managed to arrive in New York within 40 days from when SUNY first proposed the program to Mme Liu Yandong, State Councilor of China. This is a wonderful example of the efficient cooperation between China and the U.S., showing how much the relationship has grown since the first group of Chinese visiting scholars arrived at New York JFK airport in 1978.

Government Support to U.S.-China Exchange

To support U.S.-China educational exchange, the two governments signed an agreement on educational exchange and cooperation under the framework of the scientific cooperation agreement between the two governments in July 1985, and renewed the same agreement in 1990, 1993, 1995 and 1998 respectively. The two governments agreed to encourage and support individual exchange of students, teachers, lecturers, and scholars; as well as direct exchange between institutions, universities and other organizations.

U.S. Secretary of Education Mr. Richard Riley visited China in 2000, the first time in American history that a U.S. Secretary of Education had visited the country. The visit also made history in U.S.-China educational cooperation, resulting in the signing of the first agreement on educational exchange and cooperation not under the scientific cooperation agreement framework. This agreement aimed at broadening U.S.-China educational exchange programs in all academic areas, including the humanities, natural sciences, and social sciences. Mme Chen Zhili, the Chinese Minister of Education, paid a return visit to the United States the same year, the first to the U.S. by a Chinese Minister of Education in 15 years. These senior-level visits sent out the message of government support for a friendly and cooperative educational relationship.

This education agreement was renewed in 2006, and was one of the most important agreements signed between the two governments during Chinese President Hu Jintao's state visit to the United States. When addressing students at Yale University, President Hu Jintao showed his great support for U.S.-China educational exchange by asserting that "cultural, educational and youth exchange is the bridge to mutual understanding and friendship between our two peoples and is an important force to promote the healthy and stable development of U.S.-China relations." He then invited 100 students from Yale University to visit China as his guests.

To further educational cooperation at all levels, Margaret Spellings, Secretary of Education, visited China the following November together with Assistant Secretary of State Dina Powell and twelve U.S. university presidents. The delegation met with Chinese Premier Wen Jiabao and delegation members had fruitful discussions with their counterparts in China. An MOU was signed to ensure the continued development of U.S.-China educational exchange. Premier Wen Jiabao commented on the U.S.-China education exchange as one of the most important parts of China-U.S. relations.

Government Supported Cooperative Programs

Government supported programs have played a very important role in the development of U.S.-China educational exchange. Profiles of four government supported programs follow.

China-U.S. Fulbright Program

In the past 30 years of the China-U.S. Fulbright program, 591 Chinese scholars have conducted research in U.S. universities, 394 American lecturers have come to Chinese universities to teach, and the number of participating Chinese universities has expanded significantly, according to Ministry of Education statistics. The Fulbright-supported scholars are greatly respected for being selected as Fulbrighters, and the program is very influential in China. The program has contributed tremendously to the development of research in the social sciences at Chinese universities.

The Fulbright Program has been expanded in the past few years. The funding model for Chinese scholars was changed in 2004 into co-funding shared by both governments, and the number of scholars that could be supported each year doubled. The name of the program changed from the U.S. Fulbright Program to "China-U.S. Fulbright Program." Sub-programs have been expanded in recent years, including "Foreign Language Teaching Assistant" and "PhD Dissertation Research Program."

E-Language Learning System

The "E-language Learning System" is a program jointly financed and run by the two ministries of education to promote opportunities to learn each other's languages online. Experts from both sides worked closely together to develop English and Chinese language learning programs, and to provide assistance to schools in China and the U.S. The Chengo (Chinese and English on the Go) Chinese language learning system is being used by 15,000 students in 20 U.S. states. The program may help U.S. students begin learning the Chinese language in the absence of enough qualified Chinese language teachers.

U.S.-China Friendship Volunteers Program

The first group of American volunteers to arrive in China as part of this program started their teaching mission in Sichuan Province. The volunteers mainly teach English in schools and universities in remote areas of China. Since the establishment of the program in 1993, 485 American volunteers have worked in 67 schools in the provinces of western China as teachers of English or other subjects. These teachers overcame many difficulties and were devoted to their work despite the poor conditions of the teaching environment, making great contributions to the local regions.

The Senior Leadership Program

This program provides opportunities to top Chinese university leaders to spend three weeks at Yale University to discuss the administration of universities. A similar program also took place at Michigan University and Rice University in previous years. About 200 Chinese university leaders participated in the program, which strengthened the ties and relationships between universities in both countries.

There are many other cooperative government programs such as the Advanced Placement course and exam, the Eisenhower Exchange Fellowships, and others, all of which are important to U.S.-China exchange.

Best Practices in U.S.-China Exchange

Given that U.S.-China exchange is the world's most important bilateral educational exchange relationship, there are many forms of educational cooperation between the two countries. The U.S. has remained the first choice as an international education destination for Chinese students. Many agreements for student and faculty exchange, research collaboration and joint degree programs have been signed between universities from both countries. Scholarships from different sources enable large numbers of Chinese and American students to study in each other's home countries. Joint research projects bring scientists from both sides even closer together, and some joint or dual degree programs also help deepen ties between universities.

CSC Scholarship Programs

In 2007, over 3,000 students and scholars studied or carried out research in U.S. universities or research institutes under CSC scholarship programs. They went under different programs with different purposes. 2,097 PhD students under CSC's graduate study abroad program went to 291 U.S. universities and research institutes for further study. This accounts for 50% of all the Ph.D. students CSC sponsored to study abroad in 2007. The ties built through these students will further strengthen academic links between their home institutions in China and institutions in the U.S.

The CSC-co-funded Ph.D. programs with Yale University and Harvard University and the postdoctoral program with Harvard University have served as examples for more structured cooperative programs. For instance, the CSC-Yale World Leaders Program in Bio-medical Science is designed specially to train future world leaders in bio-medical science, and the two sides have worked closely together on the selection and management of the program.

The CSC sponsored the Professional Development Program of University Science Teachers, which worked with the University of California, San Diego (UCSD) and the University of Illinois at Urbana-Champaign (UIUC) to provide training to Chinese university science teachers in teaching methodology and new techniques for teaching science at the university level. The Chinese teachers are provided with access to teaching opportunities and discussions at the department of the host university that corresponds to their department at the home university. They are also provided with intensive English language training to enable them to use English as the language of instruction when teaching their own classes when they return home.

Among the American students studying in China in 2007, 103 did so under Chinese government scholarship programs. The duration of study for Chinese government-sponsored students ranges from several months to a few years. CSC also works with multinational companies on their philanthropic programs in China. IBM, GE, HP and other companies all have established their scholarship programs in China to enhance the success of students of IT and other fields.

In the past three years, together with Woodrow Wilson National Fellowship Foundation and Washington University in St. Louis, CSC organized three International Graduate Scholarship Conferences and brought thirty American and fifty Chinese universities together to discuss issues of mutual interest. The U.S. universities met with students from all around China to brief them about the U.S. higher education system and opportunities to study in U.S. universities. The conferences were well received by both sides and a fourth one was held in Beijing in October 2008.

University Linkage Programs

Many agreements have been signed between American and Chinese universities. Apart from student/faculty exchange, there are joint programs, joint research projects and many other forms of collaboration. The Chinese National Committee for Academic Degrees recently approved a proposal for a joint degree program between

Peking University and Georgia Technical University. This is the first agreement to allow two universities to put their official stamps on one degree in the history of China-U.S. educational exchange and represents significant progress in cooperative efforts to train Ph.D. students.

Five days after the massive earth quake that hit Sichuan Province on May 12, 2008, a representative of California State University arrived in Sichuan and discussed with Sichuan University, their close partner in China, how California State University could offer help to people in the affected regions. Based on the discussion, a group of experts from California arrived two weeks later in Sichuan to study the nature of the quake and to discuss how they could work with Sichuan University and the local government to try to solve some of the problems. This was based on close ties established between Sichuan University and California State University.

By the end of 2007, 39 Confucius Institutes had been established in 37 U.S. universities in 30 states to offer Chinese language teaching programs. About 100 volunteer Chinese language teachers are sent by Hanban (National Office for the Promotion of Chinese Language Teaching) to teach in U.S. universities and schools every year. The Chinese language is gradually becoming one of the most popular foreign languages for American students.

Conclusion

Mme Chen Zhili, the former Minister of Education of China (1998-2003) and current State Councilor (2003-2008), expressed her view of China-U.S. educational exchange as the most important bilateral educational exchange relationship when she met with U.S. Secretary of Education Margaret Spellings. All forms of educational exchange have yielded productive results, and both sides have benefited greatly from the exchanges. In China's process of building world-class universities, such exchange will continue to play a visible role. All Chinese universities wish more than ever to be open to the outside world and develop in a global environment. International cooperation will help Chinese higher education institutions face their own challenges.

Chapter Four
SCHOLARLY EXCHANGES WITH CHINA

BY DAVID B. J. ADAMS, COUNCIL FOR INTERNATIONAL EXCHANGE OF SCHOLARS,
A DIVISION OF THE INSTITUTE OF INTERNATIONAL EDUCATION

This brief examination of scholarly exchanges between China and the United States in the last three decades is primarily through the lens of the work of the Committee for Scholarly Communication with the Peoples Republic of China (CSCPRC) and the Fulbright Scholar Program. The author has drawn on published materials (see End-notes), the annual reports of the Council for International Exchange of Scholars (CIES), the reports of Fulbright Scholars and his own experience working on the Fulbright Scholar program in China for more than two decades, to sketch the history of these programs and to consider the challenges and successes in the operation of the Fulbright Scholar Program, especially with an eye to providing some insight for American institutions that contemplate establishing programs and campuses in China.

An historic agreement on educational relations between the United States and China signed in October 1978 restored academic exchanges between the two nations and established the base from which these exchanges continue to evolve. The American academic community had been preparing for this moment for more than a decade. In 1963, the National Academy of Sciences (NAS) convened the first of several meetings to explore establishing a committee to work toward the restoration of educational exchanges with China in the absence of diplomatic relations between the two countries. These discussions took on concrete form in 1966 when the Committee for Scholarly Communication with the People's Republic of China (CSCPRC) was established. While the CSCPRC would be based at the NAS, two other major American academic organizations—the Social Science Research Council (SSRC) and the American Council of Learned Societies (ACLS)—were equal sponsoring partners. Throughout its existence, the CSCPRC has made major contributions to fulfilling the promise of the 1978 agreement.*

During President Nixon's visit to China in 1972, the two governments agreed in principle to initiate an exchange of academic delegations, and between 1972 and 1979 when diplomatic relations were normalized a total of 73 academic delegations were ex-

* The author is particularly indebted to Mary Brown Bullock for permission to present a condensed version of material contained in her essay, "Mission Accomplished: The Influence of the CSCPRC on Educational Relations with China," Cheng Li, ed., *Bridging Minds across the Pacific: U.S.-China Educational Exchanges, 1978-2003* (Lanham, Maryland: Lexington Books, 2005). Thanks also to the editor and publisher of the cited volume.

changed. The programs of each year's 5-7 member delegations were the result of intense negotiations. Members of the delegations were drawn from a variety of disciplines, and they explored a wide range of topics from seismology and herbal pharmacology to early childhood education and Chinese painting. Because they appeared to be most promising for collaborative research, medical, agricultural and earth sciences received particular attention. The Chinese delegations were heavily weighted towards cutting edge science and applied technology, anticipating the field of study preferences of the Chinese students soon to arrive in the United States. Some American China specialists got their first look at China as escorts for the delegations. In addition to providing an introduction to the underdeveloped Chinese research institutes and a few universities, the reports increased American knowledge of the state of Chinese science. They also established collaborative research agendas for the future.

Focus on Research: CSCPRC Activities after 1978

During the 1970s, proposals to establish reciprocal exchanges of students were unsuccessful, but that quickly changed with the conclusion of the 1978 agreement. Once the agreement was concluded, it became clear that China had a long term vision of educating its best and brightest abroad. In addition, China indicated that it wanted to base future exchanges on the model established by exchanges with the U.S., such as the Boxer Indemnity Scholarships, that had taken place in the early 20th century. This represented a departure from the tightly structured, balanced model of China's exchanges with the Soviet Union.

Under the agreement, the sending of Chinese students and scholars to the United States would be a decentralized process, with American universities agreeing to evaluate the credentials of the Chinese. In addition, under the agreement, Chinese students and scholars were eligible for American institutional scholarships. This has continued to some extent, but not on the same scale as in the early days of the program. The agreement anticipated that there would be more or less the same number of scholars moving in each direction, but from the outset there have been many more Chinese students and scholars coming to the United States than American scholars and students going to China. On the student side, this imbalance is beginning to improve with a significant increase in the last five years in the number of American students going to China. When the Fulbright Program began awarding grants to Chinese students and scholars, the Ministry of Education and individual universities played a key role in the selection process. This changed in the last decade when the U.S. Embassy in Beijing and the China Scholarship Council became the key institutions in the selection of the Chinese students and scholars to receive Fulbright grants.

China did, however, insist on a centralized management process for Americans studying or doing research in China, and the Ministry of Education (MOE) was assigned this role. The CSCPRC assumed primary responsibility for administering the National Program for Advanced Study in China (the "National Program"). Between

1979 and 1996, with funding from the National Science Foundation, the National Endowment for the Humanities (NEH), the Department of Education and the United States Information Agency, the CSCPRC sent over 700 American scholars to China for sustained study and research. The majority were China specialists but some significant natural science research projects also had their start in this program. The work done by these scholars, many of whom came from liberal arts colleges and regional universities, redefined all fields of enquiry on China.

When American scholars and students sought research opportunities in locales and institutions with which the MOE had no connection, and because Chinese universities and research institutions did not have any experience with the kinds of research demands that Americans would make for access to library archives, population groups or field research, it became clear that representation from an organization on the American side was needed in China. In 1985 the CSCPRC received permission from American and Chinese officials to open an independent office in China sponsored by the Chinese Academy of Sciences to coordinate placement of all National Program students and scholars in China. During the 1980s a significant amount of the CSCPRC Beijing office's attention was given to gaining American research access to China. When Chinese institutions and government officials had earlier blocked some American social scientists from entering China, President Carter brought this up in discussions with Deng Xiaoping in 1979 and soon all initial projects were approved.

In 1980, with funding from the Henry Luce Foundation, the Starr Foundation and NEH, the CSCPRC established the Visiting Scholar Program, enabling senior scholars from each side to spend a short period in each other's countries and thereby introducing leading Chinese and American intellectuals to each other. The relationship grew in the 1980s with the addition of academic conferences and the creation of standing bilateral working groups. With assistance from the Ford Foundation, the CSCPRC established working groups in economics, law, international relations and sociology. The conferences and working groups introduced American academics to the new graduate training programs and research projects created by the Chinese and introduced Chinese to scholarly trends in the United States and Western Europe.

When academic relations with China in the 1980s expanded to direct university-to-university relations, the CSCPRC provided consultation to these emerging programs through the U.S.-China Education Clearinghouse. Its quarterly publication, *The China Exchange News*, reported on university programs and provided overviews of exchange developments in different disciplines as well as updates on developments in Chinese education policies. The CSCPRC also worked with the World Bank-funded Chinese University Development Project and spearheaded multiple phases of ongoing World Bank support for higher education in China.

The Tiananmen Incident disrupted academic exchanges temporarily in 1989 but the CSCPRC's work resumed shortly thereafter. In 1991 the CSCPRC was renamed the Committee for Scholarly Communication with China (CSCC); the National Program for Advanced Study and Research continued and remained the premier exchange program with China. The Visiting Scholars Program was re-named the Chinese Fellowships for Scholarly Development. Through the 1980s and early 1990s, the range and scope of Sino-American academic exchanges expanded significantly and by the mid-1990s U.S.-China scholarly relations had become a sophisticated, pluralistic collection of university, government agency and foundation programs.

Two aspects of the evolving bilateral relationship over which the CSCPRC presided merit particular note: 1) the respective roles of the non-profit sector and of the U.S. government, and 2) the role and importance of an interdisciplinary alliance. Even though the CSCPRC was dependent on the U.S. government in a variety of ways—most importantly for funding and communication of messages to the Chinese government—it was fundamentally an independent scholarly organization with its own intellectual agenda and the ability to choose participants in the programs it administered. Its independence was possible because of its multiple sources of funding, the international reputation of its leadership (which included two Nobel Prize winners) and the stature of its sponsoring organizations. The fact that the National Academy of Sciences was the core sponsor and home base for CSCPRC was particularly important because in addition to its international prestige it was experienced in establishing scientific ties with the USSR, Eastern Europe and developing countries, and it was also accustomed to working in partnership with the U.S. Government. The SSRC and ACLS were equally respected organizations with a broad national base and a commitment to promotion of China studies as part of their core missions, as well as to scholarly initiatives in a wide variety of traditional social science and humanistic disciplines.

During the 1970s and 80s the commonalities shared by natural scientists regardless of nationality made it easier for them to establish solid substantive relationships with Chinese colleagues than it was for social scientists and humanists. This was not simply a matter of different intellectual perspectives. It was also related to the policies of the Chinese government, which had given strong support to the sciences during the Mao years but not to other disciplines. Thus, there was virtually no infrastructure for academic exchanges in the social sciences and humanities in China. The social scientists and humanists working with the CSCPRC quickly recognized that it was essential to move beyond individual research projects toward the establishment of standing groups and workshops and conferences in a wide variety of disciplines. The resulting collaborations contributed to the resurgence of the social science and humanist disciplines in China and improved emerging bilateral relations in those fields.

The CSCPRC's ties to Chinese governmental bodies were complex and changed as China changed. In the 1970s, the Scientific and Technical Association of the Peoples Republic of China (STAPRC)—a mass organization rather than a core Chinese agency or institution—was the CSCPRC's Chinese counterpart. Although the STAPRC continued to be the designated counterpart, the CSCPRC increasingly worked more directly with four Chinese government bodies: the Chinese Academy of

Sciences, the Chinese Academy of Social Sciences, the Ministry of Education, and to a lesser extent the Ministry of Science and Technology. A core cadre of Chinese scholars and staff in these key organizations came to believe in the joint enterprise and worked hard to insulate American students and scholars from the political pressures and changes in China. This advocacy was an essential element in the expansion of academic ties between the two countries.

The CSCPRC played a key role during the transitional period, as American and Chinese scholars and institutions laid the foundations for a mature and pluralistic relationship. While the CSCPRC model is no longer needed in U.S.-China educational relations, the primary value that infused it—a belief in the transformative power of educational relations between different societies—has never been more important.

Focus on Teaching: the Resumption of the Fulbright Program

The Fulbright Program's core value was similar—to increase mutual understanding among peoples and nations through academic exchanges. However, when the Fulbright Program was re-opened in China in 1980 after an almost three decade break, the Fulbright Scholar Program had a different focus than the programs managed by the CSCPRC—teaching rather than research. In 1980 the first Fulbright Scholar lecturers went to China. In the next five years, the number of lecturers increased rapidly, more disciplines became involved, the relation of the grantees to Chinese host institutions changed and their geographic distribution expanded. The Fulbright Scholar program would add a research component in 2000 by incorporating the National Program on Advanced Study and Research in China.

The eleven American Fulbright Scholars who went to universities in Beijing, Shanghai and Nanjing in 1980-81 worked with English language teachers from all over China. They also provided information on American literature, history and culture to enrich the English language programs. The next year five grantees taught English and seven taught American history and literature. In 1982-83, Teaching English as a Foreign Language was dropped from the program, and business management, economics, law and political science were added. In addition, the Fulbright grantees were integrated into regular university departments instead of being isolated in separate English teaching units. Journalism and library science were added to the program in 1984-85. By 1985-86 the number of grantees had grown to 26.

In those early years, some grantees noted that while their relationships with their students and faculty were good, there was little opportunity to get to know Chinese faculty and students outside the classroom. Some grantees reported that they were well received by their institutions and had become more closely integrated into their departments, but others thought they were underutilized by their hosts. In this respect, the experience of the Fulbright grantees seems to have differed from that of foreign experts (i.e., contract teachers hired by Chinese institutions) who found that Chinese students made considerable demands on their time outside the classroom. While some grantees reported that there were sometimes misunderstandings about grading policies, most grantees would have concurred with the observations of a 1986-87 grantee in an article in *China Exchange News* that he had been given a free hand in teaching matter and style of instruction.

In January 1983, the American Fulbright professors met for two days with representatives of the United States Information Agency (USIA) and the Chinese Ministry of Education to assess their experiences and to share their observations about working in Chinese institutions. They reported that even though the quality of their teaching appointments varied from university to university, assignment to university departments was the best way for Chinese faculty and students to benefit from the presence of Fulbright scholars. In the following years, Chinese universities began to make fuller use of the Fulbrighters. Despite the turmoil resulting from student demonstrations in 1986-87, grantees reported much greater support and cooperation from their host institutions than in previous years.

Several important and lasting additions to the lecturing program in the 1980s increased opportunities for exchange of ideas between Chinese and American scholars. In 1983-84 arrangements were made for grantees to give occasional lectures at universities other than their host institution. In 1988-89 the U.S. Embassy provided support for a three-day symposium on American literature in China. Later that year there were also conferences on law and on economics. Conferences with varied foci have continued over the past two decades.

The Tiananmen Incident interrupted the growing relationship between the Chinese and American academic communities; and later in the summer the Chinese government announced the suspension of the Fulbright Program. The interruption was brief and the program resumed functioning in the 1990-91 academic year.

In these early years, U.S. grantees faced difficulties in obtaining sufficient advance information about their courses, their students' level of English fluency and subject knowledge, and the daily challenges of living and teaching in China. Despite these challenges, most Fulbrighters returned to the United States with a strong sense of personal and professional accomplishment and with a continuing fascination and affection for China and its people. Many of them established lasting ties with their Chinese colleagues and institutions and some facilitated institutional exchanges. The final report of a grantee in American history sums up well the sentiment of hundreds U.S. Fulbright alumni in China. His Fulbright year was, he wrote, "rich in experiences, rich in new places visited, rich in new acquaintances and rich in better understanding of this vast nation. China is not without its difficulties, but my Fulbright experience was well worth what seemed to some to be a risk."

Meanwhile, Chinese Fulbright Scholars began coming to the United States. Most came to do research in American history and American literature, but a smaller number came under the Scholar-in-Residence (SIR) Program to teach Chinese history and culture. These lecturers provided American scholars and students with their first face-to-face contact with China. One of the most notable was Ying Ruocheng, a leading Chinese actor, who in 1982 taught courses on Chinese theater and organized a production of an English-language version of a modern Chinese classic play that was entered in the 1983 American College Theater competition. He and his wife gave numerous lectures and radio-TV interviews at a variety of universities. Before returning to China, Ying met with playwright Arthur Miller and completed plans for Miller to direct a production of *Death of a Salesman* in Beijing.

Ongoing Academic Exchange Research: Challenges and Opportunities

In 2000, the National Program on Advanced Study and Research in China was formally brought under the auspices of the Fulbright Program. At that time, the Council on International Exchange of Scholars (CIES), a division of the Institute of International Education (IIE), assumed responsibility for administering these Fulbright Scholar grants, and IIE was given responsibility for administering the American Fulbright Student grants, paralleling the administrative role both these organizations have fulfilled for the worldwide Fulbright program on behalf of the U.S. Department of State since the Fulbright Program's founding in 1946.

The reports of most of the American Fulbright research scholars, especially in the last five years, have been positive. Some of them reported experiencing a "spirit of friendship and collaboration" in their interactions with Chinese scholars and a sense that the barriers between the Chinese and American communities were being reduced. Alumni in a variety of disciplines make particular note in their final reports of the importance of the assistance provided to them and their projects by Chinese scholars. For example, one scholar wrote that several Chinese experts helped to guide him through some initial difficulties and "opened up new and exciting opportunities for future collaborations." Another American scholar appreciated the important contribution made to his research by Chinese colleagues through informal conversation, networking assistance, and referral to work by Chinese scholars in similar disciplines. Their shared research interests and the ability of most American grantees to communicate in Mandarin made it possible for these Fulbrighters to establish a different kind of relationship with the Chinese scholarly community than the lecturers.

The collaborative spirit noted above has taken on concrete manifestations that suggest a framework or strategy for continued strengthening of relations between Chinese and American scholars who specialize in studying China. The experience of one scholar who was working on a controversial subject is illustrative. Her research, she notes, was facilitated by becoming integrated into research projects being carried out by Chinese scholars. This close collaboration with Chinese students and scholars who were working on projects funded by the Chinese government enabled her to gain access to data that would have been otherwise unavailable to her. The added benefit was the insight she gained from working with scholars who were studying a similar topic but from a different perspective. Drawing on the networks that she built, she has begun to plan some joint projects between American and Chinese scholars.

Another Fulbright researcher facilitated her own research and contributed to the development of China's research capacity by training anthropology graduate students to conduct a survey and to code open-ended questions, thereby introducing them to quantitative research from start to finish. She later returned to present the findings from her preliminary analysis of the data which she considered an important and essential way of fulfilling her obligations to her new Chinese colleagues and graduate student assistants. A grantee in the field of archaeology who also trained students to assist him with his work considered this an investment in what he plans to be a long term collaboration with China.

While some of the problems experienced by American scholars such as gaining access to archives and libraries are less common, some other problems have persisted. There have been several instances of host institutions withdrawing offers of visa sponsorship on the eve of the grantee's departure from the United States. Some grantees report that their host institutions were unwilling or unable to arrange interviews for them or to assist them in gaining access to archives or library resources. Another area of concern is the sometimes sizeable affiliation fees charged by host institutions, with few services provided. There needs to be provision for scholar status for academics from abroad rather than the student status that is often assigned, resulting in problems gaining access to research facilities.

Challenges in the Lecturing Program

The lecturing part of the Fulbright Scholar Program in China has presented a different set of challenges. The interim and final reports of Fulbright lecturers over the twenty-eight year history of the Fulbright lecturing program in China suggest that, overall, there have been considerable improvements. Positive improvements have occurred in areas such as classroom and housing facilities, library resources and access to them, English language abilities of students and the level and quality of assistance provided by universities' international offices (*waiban*). On the other hand, there continues to be a significant level of continuity in grantees' disappointment about the level and extent of their interactions with Chinese counterparts and the lack of opportunity to get to know them. In many cases, they quickly recognize that their students will be their primary point of contact with China. While some recent grantees report receiving warm welcomes from their colleagues and assistance in a variety of ways, others write that their relations with colleagues were cordial but that interactions were limited. One grantee compared his experience at his host institution with what he observed on other campuses and concluded, not surprisingly, that the kind of reception that a grantee receives is determined to a significant degree by the value that the administration of an institution places on international contacts and collegial exchange. Other grantees have attributed the lack of engagement to their colleagues' lack of English language capability, or their perception that that their English language abilities are insufficient to build a relationship with the visiting American scholar. Others suggest that Chinese academics are very busy in their institutions and also engaged in a variety of income earning activities beyond their campuses, and thus do not have time to devote to building relationships with American scholars.

Over the program's history, grantees have talked much about the quality of service provided by the international offices (*waiban*) at their institutions. In the early years, complaints were almost universal, but as the quality of personnel in those offices has risen, the number of complaints has declined. Many grantees find the *waiban* office helpful and welcoming, but others continue to report that these offices provide little help or guidance. In contrast with the early days of the program, when grantees found classroom facilities poor and lacking in basic teaching tools (e.g., good quality chalk), many recent grantees report teaching in very up-to-date "smart classrooms" where every student is sitting in front of a computer. A grantee who has been affiliated with the same institution twice reported that its classrooms have been refurbished and upgraded and equipped with excellent stand alone instructional technology. Another grantee, however, found himself in a classroom with old hardwood desks and benches and a seminar room that was "stark, unclean, uncomfortable and uninspiring." There has been improvement in the quality of libraries as well as access to them for visiting lecturers and their students, but grantees continue to report problems gaining library privileges at their host institutions. This is compensated for in part by the first-rate public libraries found in Beijing and Shanghai, some of which are open to foreigners.

Grantees continue to report significant variation in the quality of their students, especially their English-language proficiency. One grantee found that with few exceptions his students were thoughtful, sensitive, attentive and hard-working and possessed excellent reading, writing and speaking skills in English, but another reported that while all of his students worked very hard, they varied in their English proficiency, which necessitated spending considerable time on class preparations and reducing assignments.

Over the years, lecturers have also confronted challenges that are rooted in Chinese culture and tradition. Two of the most important are: 1) the traditional Chinese perspective that education is primarily about transmitting a body of knowledge rather than the learning of critical and analytical skills; and 2) the collective nature of Chinese society and culture. One law professor was struck by his students' communal approach to learning, in contrast to Americans' individualistic approach. He also found his students reticent to speak in class, which he attributed to a variety of factors including a reluctance to "show off" in front of others and a lack of confidence in their English language skills. He also attributed it to a more fundamental difference—an academic tradition that does not include training in critically examining information.

In addition to their classroom work, American Fulbright lecturers have contributed to Chinese universities in other ways. During the early years, in the absence of appropriate reading materials, many of the grantees worked with Chinese colleagues to develop them. A recent graduate reports that his lecture notes and PowerPoint presentations for his Strategic Management and Research Methods courses were disseminated to faculty who may teach these courses in the future. Another grantee incorporated Digital Video Conferences with senior non-profit manager into one of his courses which were recorded and they provided the basis for a new master's level program in the field. Several professors of American literature who are also poets have introduced Chinese poetry to an English speaking audience through their translations undertaken with their Chinese students and colleagues.

New Partnerships with Chinese Universities

The establishment of the Nanjing University-Johns Hopkins University Center for Chinese and American Studies in the 1980s was a harbinger of the next and ongoing phase in Sino-American academic exchanges. From the outset the institution has been bi-national in every respect—student body, faculty and administration. For much of its history, the Center offered only certificate programs, but in the last two years a master's program has been introduced. Its success and mode of operation bear careful study by other American institutions seeking to establish programs or campuses in China.

When the Chinese government began to allow foreign colleges and universities to establish formal partnerships with Chinese institutions in 1995, universities all over the world, attracted by China's growing and continuing educational needs, quickly began to establish hundreds of programs. These programs are of varied quality, and have taken a variety of approaches including joint degrees, degrees from the American institution and the so-called "sandwich programs" in which students who receive part of their education in China and part of it in the United States get either a joint degree or a degree from the Chinese or the American institution. While some American institutions will succeed in establishing programs in partnership with premier institutions, other will find that they have partnered with institutions where the students are mediocre and lack sufficient English skills. American institutions also sometimes discover that the facilities being provided by the partner institution are inadequate or unsatisfactory. Things moved one step further in 2005 when the University of Nottingham became the first Western university to open a campus in China.

Many institutions that have established or tried to establish Chinese campuses have encountered a number of problems that have been examined in recent articles in the American higher education press. Two of the biggest challenges American institutions face are: 1) the relatively weak English language skills of the student pool; and 2) difficulty in staffing the campuses in China, with an ongoing challenge of persuading American faculty members to relocate to China. American institutions (and their Chinese hosts) quickly discover that hiring and retaining expats can be expensive, and thus they end up relying heavily on locally hired faculty. American institutions considering establishing a campus or a program in China should also consider the cultural and social challenges of delivering American-style education to students educated in a very different learning tradition in which students are socialized to value being part of the group rather than standing out as an individual. The Chinese Ministry of Education has also begun to give more attention to the challenges inherent in programs offered by foreign institutions. These overseas campuses can expect closer scrutiny and the development and enforcement of more stringent standards.

Two factors stand out as essential to the early success of the CSCPRC and the ongoing success of the Fulbright Program in China: carefully selecting quality grantees, and the importance of operating within the framework of the Chinese academic environment. In the past, American scholars in China may have sought by example and persuasion to show their Chinese students and colleagues an alternative approach to education, but in the final analysis they were operating within the Chinese academic framework. In contrast, today U.S. scholars and institutions operating in China often come with the goal of delivering American-style programs, and their Chinese counterparts are asking for such programs as well. To offer a higher chance of success in these ventures in China, American and Chinese institutions alike would be wise to consider how to overcome the challenges posed by such an approach. The most promising might be contextualization of these programs, i.e., adjusting teaching styles to be more compatible with the previous educational experience of Chinese students and to introduce Chinese subject matter into the courses.

Viewed in a longer historical perspective, the major advances in scholarly communication with China are an investment in mutual understanding, and that understanding will eventually change both cultures. Many of the Chinese students and scholars who have studied abroad have returned to China with an increased appreciation for the learning traditions present in Western intellectual inquiry. They have begun to apply these tools very effectively in their own context, and they are ideal collaborators for American institutions wishing to develop new programming in China.

NOTES

CIES and Fulbright Scholar Reports

The Annual Reports of the Council for International Exchange of Scholars (CIES) provided very useful information about the Fulbright Scholar Program in China in its first decade. The final reports of Fulbright Scholar grantees were also an important source of information.

Three published sources were important in informing my discussion of the CSCPRC and academic exchanges with China between 1978 and 1989.

Mary Brown Bullock, "Mission Accomplished: The Influence of the CSCPRC on Educational Relations with China," Cheng Li, ed., *Building Bridges Across the Pacific: China Educational Exchanges, 1978-2003* (Lanham, Maryland: Lexington Books, 2005).

Ruth Hayhoe, *China's Universities and the Open Door* (M.E. Sharpe, Armonk, NY, 1989).

David M. Lampton, et al., *A Relationship Restored: Trends in U.S.-China Educational Exchanges, 1978-1984* (National Academy Press, 1986).

Articles on the efforts of American institutions to establish programs and campuses in China consulted include:

Lisa Chiu, "UW Declines Invitation to Create Campus in China," *Seattle Times*, June 30, 2006.

Paul Mooney, "An American College in China Struggles to Deliver," *Chronicle of Higher Education*, May 2, 2008.

New York Institute of Technology (NYIT) press release, "New York Institute of Technology Opens American-Style University in China."

Osman Ozturgut, "Teaching West in the East: An American University in China," *International Journal of Teaching and Learning in Higher Education*, Vol. 19, No. 3, 2007.

Edgar A. Porter, *Foreign Teachers in China: Old Problems for a New Generation, 1979-1989* (Greenwood Press, New York, 1990), 56.

Elizabeth Redden, "The Phantom Campus in China," *Inside HigherEd*, February 12, 2008.

Craig Simons, "American Universities Flock to China," Cox News Service, July 1, 2007.

Chapter Five

U.S.-CHINA STUDENT AND TEACHER EXCHANGE PROGRAMS: DEVELOPING UNDERSTANDING IN A GLOBAL AGE

BY MARGOT E. LANDMAN, NATIONAL COMMITTEE ON U.S.-CHINA RELATIONS AND CHARLOTTE S. MASON, CHINA EXCHANGE INITIATIVE

Today we live in a global community, where all countries must work as partners to promote peace and prosperity and to resolve international problems. One of the surest ways to develop and strengthen such partnerships is through international educational programs.

President William Jefferson Clinton, November 2000

The exchange was, quite simply, the most important experience of my life. It provided me with a base for understanding China that has been crucial to my study of China [ever since]. The exchange provided me not only with friends for life, but also with a passion for China that I know will last a lifetime.

Ben Liebman, 1986 Newton exchange student;
currently professor of law and director of the
Center for Chinese Legal Studies at Columbia Law School

We have heard presidents, prime ministers, CEOs, foreign ministers, and professionals in numerous fields speak about the transformative experience of educational exchange and its positive impact on relations between countries, on strategic planning, on problem solving, and on the global marketplace. We listened to the 45-minute speech given at Beijing University in April 2008 by the prime minister of Australia *in Mandarin*, which he learned as a student living in Beijing, and honed when he served as Australia's ambassador to China. Communicating with others in their native language is a priceless tool of diplomacy. The United States needs leaders with diplomatic skills, experience, and breadth of mind, all of which may be acquired through carefully designed international educational sojourns. We have listened to exchange teachers and students reminisce about teaching and learning abroad. While learning about others, they also clearly learn about themselves and gain new perspectives.

Teachers touch many students' lives and provide the horizontal rationale for exchange. Upon return to their home country, teachers spread their new knowledge and perspective throughout the profession of teaching, and to students. They enter the classroom with renewed energy; they contribute to their school system's curriculum reform and improvement; and they make presentations at professional conferences. High school students stand at the very beginning of long, productive careers and provide the vertical rationale for exchange. They may go into careers they never anticipated, using knowledge of Chinese language and culture acquired during an exchange and deepened in college and graduate school. Exchange students and teachers touch the lives of many others around them. Their broad perspectives, authentic cultural understandings, warm intercultural friendships, and self-awareness are desperately needed in our interconnected world and should be highly valued in our country in all fields of work and study.

Goals and Initiatives for Secondary School Partnerships

When the U.S.-China Teachers Exchange Program was established by the American Council of Learned Societies (ACLS)[1] and the China Education Association for International Exchange (CEAIE) in 1995 with generous funding from the Freeman Foundation, the American and Chinese partners had several goals: the Chinese schools and educational authorities hoped to improve the English language proficiency and understanding of American culture of Chinese teachers of English, as well as their knowledge of innovative teaching techniques. Their American counterparts looked to broaden student understanding of and openness to the world, to begin or strengthen Chinese language instruction, and to improve teaching about China across the curriculum. Individual participants would grow professionally and personally through spending a year in the host country.

In the 13 years since the inception of the program, 280 Chinese teachers from 86 schools in 24 cities across China have come to the United States. They have been placed in 51 districts – more than 100 schools – in 15 states ranging from Maine to Oregon, Florida to Wisconsin, and Texas to Colorado. 100 American teachers have gone to seven provinces in China. We estimate that each American participant teaches approximately 5,600 Chinese students each year (Chinese classes are huge by American standards, ranging from some 40 to 70 students per class). Because American classes are much smaller, each Chinese educator teaches approximately 2,400 American students annually. Over time, tens of thousands of students are directly exposed to the authentic experience of learning from a native of a foreign country. As some third graders in Miami recently noted with excitement, they were taught by a "real Chinese person" for the very first time. Colleagues, parents, community members, and friends are also affected by the program through formal presentations and information conversations. Not only are the numbers significant, but so is the quality; all participating teachers are experienced professionals dedicated to education and to the idea that improving communication and understanding between Chinese and Americans is critical.

In executing the program, some of these goals have been met; others have proved more elusive as constraints on both sides have limited possibilities. In the United States,[2] financial realities have meant that many school districts have been unable to expand foreign language offerings. The increasing emphasis on testing in core subjects also means little time for foreign languages, and even social studies – an obvious place in the curriculum for teaching about China – suffers under pressure to raise scores in reading and math. If the exams do not cover China, most teaching will not, either. In addition, the decentralization of American education into many different state systems with heavy emphasis on local planning and leadership leaves little centralized support for policy, curriculum development, and financing for international exchange, whereas the centrally organized Chinese educational system is more clearly able to articulate the value of foreign language study and international exchange for its students and teachers.

In many parts of the United States, however, educators understand that the rise of China means that schools must teach about China if their students are to be prepared adequately for the future. Teachers cannot teach what they do not know, so the imperative to strengthen teachers' knowledge of China has become increasingly clear. There are many ways of improving teacher knowledge – through undergraduate and graduate coursework, summer or term-time institutes, study tours, and extended sojourns in China. Programs based on all of these methods have expanded over the past decade. In addition, Chinese exchange teachers bring authenticity to efforts to expand the place of China in the American school and community—a living, breathing Chinese person from whom we can learn what life in contemporary China is all about is an incomparable resource.

Exchange programs have been a critical instrument for updating curriculum, and especially for helping to initiate Chinese language programs. Returning teachers bring back an increased understanding of modern China into their classrooms. When used strategically in school systems to review curriculum materials used in teaching about China, these teachers are invaluable at recognizing, introducing, and disseminating improved educational content.

Another important program, the China Exchange Initiative (CEI), was established in 1999 to create U.S.-China school exchange programs at the suggestion of Mr. Houghton Freeman of the Freeman Foundation, after he observed students from Newton, Massachusetts entering college East Asian studies programs, many of which were supported by the Freeman Foundation. These students spoke fluent Mandarin, took great interest in the culture and history of China, spoke lovingly about host parents and siblings in Beijing, and sought career opportunities to build on their exchange experiences. The Newton students were participants in a long-standing (and on-going) exchange program between Newton Public Schools and the Beijing Jingshan School. The relationship between the schools began in 1979 with a chance meeting of two teachers whose husbands were building a joint venture together. Deng Xiaoping himself provided the special permission required at that time to create an experimental exchange program. His rationale was that he had greatly valued his own experience as a student in France, he had grandchildren in the Jingshan School, and he hoped that Chinese students would benefit as he had from an international education experience.

Mr. Freeman wanted to ensure that students in other U.S. schools would have opportunities for U.S.-China exchange, similar to that of the Newton students. Newton remains the laboratory for the exchange programs, which CEI, working with CEAIE and provincial and municipal bureaus of education, fosters between many schools in different parts of the U.S. and China. Experience has shown that the most sustainable exchange programs occur in places where networks of school partnerships connect geographic areas, and where state governments, educational institutions, and cultural organizations value and support international educational exchange. For example, schools in Connecticut are connected to schools in Shandong Province; other partners are Indiana and Liaoning, Oklahoma and Sichuan, North Carolina and Jiangsu.

Laying the Groundwork for Education Abroad in the Secondary School Curriculum

In the spring of 2008, a panel of Newton students testified before a Newton strategic planning committee for schools in 2020. They overwhelmingly conveyed the message that they crave relevance in their education. They described the most memorable school experiences as school trips, exchange programs, and interdisciplinary classes concerned with global issues and solutions.

A high quality educational exchange program is generally integrated into a school's curriculum, especially in language, social studies, world literature, and science. If there is a strong Chinese language program already in place then a goal of the exchange program is to provide language immersion during a lengthy stay at the partner school in China, for as long as a semester. If the school does not yet have a Chinese language program, then the school visit might be as short as a week in combination with some tourism.[3] In either case, it is essential to keep the focus on the school-to-school and host family nature of the trip and not tourism. Students can be tourists at any time, but may have only one chance at such an on-the-ground, real-life immersion in another culture. When they return to China during a college junior year abroad, they report that living in a dormitory is very different from living with a host family.

It is also essential to keep the exchange equal on both sides and to maintain a tone of mutuality and respect in all communications between partner schools. Equal does not mean identical. It is possible to design an exchange in which a smaller number of visitors from one side stay longer than the larger number of visitors from the other. It is important to keep in mind that each side has to serve the best interests of the respective school and will have different goals. For the Chinese school, the most frequently stated goals are to improve the school's English language teaching, and the language and other skills of the visiting teachers and students. They want to examine pedagogy, school management, "moral education,"[4] and how American schools foster creativity. The American goals are more general: to immerse students and teachers in a rich culture and language, provide them with authentic cultural interactions, and encourage them to learn both inside and beyond the classroom. Whatever the stated goals, the experience often proves to be broader, deeper, and more transformative than anticipated, and it changes the participant forever.

It is useful for school administrators to create a context for exchange programs in order to articulate a vision for education in a global age. For example, setting up a global education task force in a school creates a context for all international programs, and indicates to the teacher/champions of the different programs that they are valued and have a visible place in the school. In schools in which French and German are still taught but increasingly in competition with Spanish for students, a global education task force can help reduce tension by uniting teachers around a common, stated school goal.

This context will also help foster the updating of curriculum, including initiating Chinese language programs and adding new units about China in social studies and world literature. The superintendent of Needham (MA) Public Schools has formed a global education committee that reviews curriculum, oversees exchange programs, and supervises a global competencies certification program. The Global Competence Program encourages students think globally through requirements including international experience, language study, service, and others. This program has both encouraged the internationalization of the curriculum and also placed students' involvement in international exchange, either as travelers or as hosts and facilitators, within the wider frame of global awareness.

The criteria for selection of American students and accompanying teachers for exchange programs need to be clear, fair, stated in writing, and compatible with the school's mission. Strategic selections benefit school systems the most. Teachers/chaperones are selected for what they can bring back to their schools and classrooms; the first choice is those who teach about China. Students are selected on the basis of their success in a pertinent course of study, especially Chinese language, world history, or Asian studies, and for such qualities as flexibility, cultural sensitivity, and a keen sense of adventure.

In order to prepare students and teachers effectively, it is important to select them several months in advance and to meet with the selected group on a regular basis for orientation. This process will prepare them to host, travel, and be hosted, assist with completion of medical and liability forms, provide a chance check insurance policies, establish rules and expectations, introduce them to the culture, and, where possible, provide intensive language classes and briefings by China specialists. (A handbook, *U.S.-China School Exchange Programs*, is available from CEI upon request.) The group should learn the host school's rules (about wearing the school uniform, maintaining haircuts, eschewing jewelry and makeup, dating, etc.), and prepare to follow them for as long as they are enrolled. Exchange students and teachers truly serve as ambassadors and need to be aware of sensitive subjects and how to handle delicate situations diplomatically. It is helpful for them to keep in mind that they are there to learn, not to proselytize (literally and figuratively).

Preparing to Welcome Chinese Exchange Teachers to U.S. Communities

As an American school contemplates inviting a Chinese exchange teacher for a year, several questions must be addressed. How will the teacher be used in the school/district?[5] How will the teacher be supported personally and professionally? What will the teacher's role in the community be? The answers will depend on the particular situation on the ground. There is enormous variation across the United States; an effective approach in one place could well be a disaster in another. In general, however, a successful exchange requires the support of someone at the district level (superintendent or associate/assistant superintendent for curriculum and instruction), one or two people in the building(s) to which the teacher is assigned (principal and department chair), and perhaps someone in the community who will help the teacher to broaden his/her circle beyond the school environment. American exchange teacher "alumni" can serve the latter role extremely well. Because they have spent a year in China, usually very warmly welcomed and supported, they are eager to reciprocate, even if the teacher in their American school or district does not come from the school in China in which they taught.

All participants in the U.S.-China Teachers Exchange Program go through a rigorous selection process. Cooperating Chinese schools are generally chosen by CEAIE in collaboration with provincial and municipal education bureaus. The schools then nominate teachers who complete a written application, which is followed up by an interview conducted in person by the Chinese and American program directors. Four criteria are considered: English proficiency, ability to speak standard Chinese (this is critical, as American students are ill-served by Chinese language instructors with strong local accents), adaptability and flexibility, and likelihood to return to China on time.[6] After teachers have been selected, they are assigned to American schools on the basis of the schools' plans for them, as well as preferences expressed by the teachers for large or medium-sized cities, small cities, suburbs, or rural areas. If there is a sister school or sister city relationship, then the teachers automatically go to the sister school or city. Both traveling teachers and host schools should prepare in advance for arrival in the United States. The program has developed guides for Chinese teachers, host schools, and host families (available on the National Committee's website, www.ncuscr.org/programs/tep). An intensive pre-departure orientation program is held in July before the teachers travel. Building on the Chinese teachers' extensive teaching experience in China (most teachers have been in the classroom for a minimum of eight years, and some for as many as 25 years), it focuses on how to teach American students as well as on classroom management, often a major issue for teachers new to the American education system.

At the same time, host schools prepare for their guest. They not only assign classes and purchase teaching materials, but they identify a mentor. It is best that the mentor be a fellow teacher, rather than an administrator, because hierarchy concerns may make it difficult for a Chinese teacher to speak openly of issues to someone perceived as a superior. They also find a host family, or make arrangements for the teachers to live in an apartment. Given that one of the goals of an exchange program is learning as much as possible about the host country and its culture, host families are generally preferable to independent apartment living. If host families cannot be found and teachers are asked to live in apartments, deliberate efforts must be made to include the exchange teachers in community activities. In one instance, the administrator responsible for the exchange teacher divided the school year into two-week segments. Every department, including administrative units and the custodial team, was assigned one two-week slot during which it was responsible for doing something social with the teacher with the goal to make the teacher feel a part of the community.

A common issue for Chinese visitors to the United States is transportation. Most teachers do not drive. This is changing, however; in recent years one or two teachers in each cohort has had a Chinese driver's license (driving in the United States requires a local license; obtain the details at the local Department of Motor Vehicles). While some take driving lessons while in the United States, most depend on public transportation or on lifts. For the students, none of whom can drive, the problems are similar, but involve the host families. They must ask their host families to help them navigate their comings and goings.

Before the Chinese exchange delegation arrives, the group must undergo a rigorous visa process. The host school sends an invitation, signed by the principal or superintendent, that includes the names, title, gender, birth date, and birth place for each member of the delegation, and an overall plan for the visit. A copy of the invitation is also sent to the U.S. Embassy or appropriate consulate[7] about ten days prior to the visa interview appointment. Only after members of the group have obtained visas may they make travel arrangements. Flexibility is required because there may be delays. Visas are occasionally denied if the consular officials believe that an applicant is a risk for non-return to China. Applicants may try again, and often succeed the second time.

It is helpful to form a China exchange committee in the school community, made up of current and former exchange students and their families, members of the faculty and administration, and interested representatives of local businesses and cultural institutions. Members of the committee provide resources and knowledge, recruit host families, and plan activities for the visitors. In order to provide a broad experience for the visitors, they draw up a calendar of activities, such as invitations to people's homes, school concerts, plays, and sports events, holiday celebrations, community events, shopping, hiking, and tickets to theater, museums, and professional sports games. During the exchange, in order to keep costs to a minimum and to provide the deepest possible cultural immersion, students are hosted by families on both sides.

Finding American host families is a job involving the whole school community, and casting a wide net ensures maximum interest. Experience shows that the key determinants of success are that the host family regularly has dinner together as a family and that they take an active interest in their guest's life. Qualified host families often self-select, because they are interested in providing a cross-cultural experience for their family or because they have a special interest in China.

Making the Most of a Chinese Teacher's Stay

At the beginning of their stay in the United States, Chinese exchange teachers need some guidance to navigate American schools effectively. Even though they are experienced teachers in China, it is helpful for them to attend programs for new teachers in the American host schools and districts. They will learn from colleagues about the issues facing all teachers in American classrooms. If Chinese language classes comprise the bulk of the teaching assignment, they should be given the textbooks they will be asked to use as early as possible.

Experience has taught that working as both a language teacher and a resource teacher is often the most effective assignment for the exchange teacher. The language classes give the teacher the sense that he/she is part of the faculty with a clearly defined goal – teaching students to speak, understand, read, and write Chinese. Acting as a resource teacher throughout the school, or in several schools within the district, allows the teacher to be more widely known, and for many more students to be exposed to the visiting teacher.

Two examples demonstrate the effectiveness of this approach. In La Crosse, Wisconsin, a small city on the Mississippi River, the exchange teachers join an American teacher of Chinese at the high school level. They teach at least three, and sometimes four, levels of Chinese each year. In addition, they visit an elementary school in the district that is part of the international school movement in the United States. They work with each kindergarten class in the school for several weeks, teaching the children about Chinese culture. They also offer after school clubs for fourth and fifth graders at the school. The specific activities of the clubs change from year to year depending on the strengths of the teachers, but may include calligraphy, *taijiquan*, cooking, and other subjects. The clubs have grown extremely popular as word about them has spread.

In Westport, Connecticut, a suburb of New York City, Chinese language instruction was added to the high school curriculum in 2005, several years after the

Teachers Exchange Program had been introduced to the district. The visiting teachers co-teach with an extremely gifted American teacher of Chinese. They also spend five weeks in each of the district's fourth grade classrooms offering a unit on geography. Part of the district's social studies curriculum, the unit strives to answer several "essential questions" about the connections between geography and culture.[8] At first, the assignment challenged the Chinese teachers. As secondary school foreign language teachers in China, they had never been asked to consider "essential questions"; nor had they ever taught geography. With support from the district, an excellent unit has developed. The fourth grade classroom teachers, elementary school principals, students, and visiting teachers are all extremely positive about the experience. Some of the students now studying Chinese at the high school level first became excited about China when they had Chinese exchange teachers in their fourth grade classrooms.

Not surprisingly, however, the biggest culture shock for any visiting teacher is undoubtedly the American classroom. In general, China is very homogeneous. The mix of races, ethnicities, and often nationalities in an American school will be quite startling. The Chinese image of "an American" is a European-American. We devote much time and effort during the pre-departure orientation program to discussion of diversity, and the importance of treating everyone, regardless of color, religion, sexual orientation, economic status, and other differences, equally and fairly. We reiterate these themes on many occasions, including at our annual mid-year conference. It is difficult to change cultural stereotypes through words; working with and teaching different kinds of people is the most effective means of opening eyes, hearts, and minds.

Exchange teachers will also probably be startled by the range of abilities in many American schools. Chinese schools are quite rigidly "tracked" and many exchange teachers come from the most selective schools with the best students, the most highly qualified teachers, and the most sophisticated equipment. They will be surprised by classes that include special education students and students headed for top American universities. They may wonder why there is just one DVD player in the entire school, rather than in each classroom. Most of all, they will be thrown by the notion that it is the teacher's responsibility to make learning fun and interesting, rather than the student's "duty" to study, regardless of his/her interests or abilities.

Although the pre-departure orientation and materials sent to the teachers in advance try to prepare them for the realities of American schools and classrooms, entering the classroom for the first time may be a rude awakening. A mentor is critical. The teacher must have someone to whom he/she can turn for suggestion. The teacher should be guided through the school's (district's) disciplinary procedures, and encouraged to seek assistance from guidance counselors, deans, and others who may be responsible for student behavior. The teacher should not feel alone in dealing with challenging students.

The first few weeks are undoubtedly the most difficult. The teacher is getting used to new students, new surroundings, new food and water – new everything! It may seem quite overwhelming. As time passes, however, the teacher adjusts, and so do the students. Incorporating some elements of the Chinese school day into the Chinese classroom in the United States may be very effective. To create an atmosphere that says, "This is a Chinese classroom," some teachers have the students rise at the beginning of class, greeting the teacher as Chinese students do. It sets a tone, saying that genuine learning is taking place. It came as quite a shock to an American observer to walk into a classroom of American juniors and seniors to find them singing "*Liang zhi Laohu*" ("Two Tigers") to the tune of "Frère Jacques," complete with the hand gestures signifying that one tiger lacks ears and the other lacks a tail! The notion that the teenagers would consider such an activity beneath them fell by the wayside because the teacher assumed that the students would follow her willingly, and the students rose to the challenge.

American students and teachers need thorough preparation to live successfully with Chinese host families. They must realize, for example, that China has a very particular food culture, in which food is both an art form and a demonstration of hospitality. Meals are served at regular times and are specially prepared for visitors. American students tend to be quite casual about food and meal times. Guests in a Chinese household must express appreciation for the food, no matter how unfamiliar it may be, and be on time for meals. In fact, it is extremely rude to be late for anything in China. Chinese host students devote a great deal of time to studying, so time for socializing with the visiting American student may be limited. Simultaneously, American students have to earn their freedoms in a Chinese household used to quite restrictive schedules. Extreme hospitality can sometimes feel like over-protection. Exchange students and teachers learn to conform to many differences in life-style.

Hosting Students at Chinese and American Schools

At the Chinese partner school, the U.S. students spend each day both in a few regular classes with their fifty to sixty Chinese classmates and also in some classes designed especially for them, including Chinese language courses. Accompanying teachers work a full schedule as English teachers ("foreign experts"), regardless of their fields at home. Generally they are asked to teach English speaking, listening, and writing skills once a week in each of the host school's English classes, leaving the grammar lessons to the Chinese teachers of English. On weekends, the host school often plans tourist expeditions for all of the visitors. During school holidays the group may travel in China after determining realistic costs and destinations.

The Chinese students in the United States are scheduled into a variety of academic and elective classes. They may feel frustrated by their inability to excel academically in a new setting, at least initially, and to make friends easily in classes that change during each period (in China the teachers, not the students, change classes). Consideration should be given to grading them on a pass/fail basis. The visiting students and teacher/chaperone are asked to make presentations about Chinese culture in classrooms at all grade levels where China is taught. Lively, interactive presentations are popular and benefit the whole school community, but some direction from a host teacher and rehearsal are necessary. Similarly, in English classes in China the Americans are often asked to read class materials, make presentations about American culture, and create skits and dialogues for use in the classes.

Because Chinese schools value exchange with U.S. counterparts and because their teachers usually teach only two classes per day, they are willing and able to provide special classes for visiting U.S. students and teachers that focus on Chinese language, history, arts, and martial arts. American schools have less flexibility in staffing, but can sometimes offer visiting Chinese students help if needed in existing ELL/ESL classes. However, Chinese junior and senior high school students generally have excellent English language skills that enable them to participate fully in many regular classes.[9] They often require no ELL services.[10]

Americans are beginning to recognize the benefits of international exchange and mastery of foreign languages, especially Mandarin, as China's international role becomes more evident. Firms that do business in China need fluent Mandarin speakers; American universities need faculty knowledgeable about China; schools and social service agencies in the United States need interpreters and translators of culture as the Chinese population in the United States grows; the diplomatic corps and military establishment seek people attuned to Chinese culture and language. Further, transnational issues in health and medicine, trade, energy security, the environment, and international relations require global solutions from people who can communicate and work together. Exchange programs at the pre-collegiate level provide a basis on which these critical skills may be built.

NOTES

[1] The program moved to the National Committee on United States – China Relations in June 2002.

[2] We will focus on the United States in this chapter; the challenges facing Chinese educators within China, and Americans teaching in Chinese schools, are in some cases quite different from educational issues in the United States.

[3] Most schools that develop exchange programs with partner schools in China seek to build Chinese language programs as a result of the student, faculty, and parent interest that grows out of the exchange.

[4] Moral education, as it is called in China, encompasses something akin to American civics. A Chinese colleague defined it as "the teaching and learning of social norms, traditions and values which help young learners grow up to be productive and patriotic citizens with a sense of social responsibility and scientific [objective] outlook on the world and life. It is a very important aspect of education in China, starting in kindergarten." Personal communication with one of the authors, August 21, 2008.

[5] The U.S.-China Teachers Exchange Program is open to public and private schools. In the public school setting, the teacher may teach in more than one school in the district; teachers at private schools work within one institution, although they may teach in the lower, middle, and upper schools over the course of the school year.

[6] Administrators of programs with China (as well as many other countries) must be aware of the possibility of overstayed visas. Not only is it illegal for program participants to stay beyond the duration of stay on their visa documents, but participants who overstay also jeopardize the future of the programs as U.S. consular authorities may be reluctant to issue visas if a program has a significant history of overstays.

[7] Each consular office has jurisdiction over the applications from a designated part of China.

[8] For example, "essential questions" in fourth grade social studies might include: "How do natural resources and technology influence the ways in which people live?" Or, "What are the identifying features of a biome and how do they affect life forms?"

[9] The national curriculum set by the Chinese Ministry of Education has English language instruction beginning in grade three. A small number of pre-schools offer English, and some elementary schools, especially those in large cities, start English in first grade.

[10] If the Chinese visitors do require English language support, it may be an issue for U.S. schools in which ESL is often oversubscribed and underfunded.

Chapter Six

COORDINATING CAMPUS-WIDE CHINA EXCHANGES: THE GEORGE MASON UNIVERSITY EXAMPLE

BY MADELYN ROSS, GEORGE MASON UNIVERSITY

For thirty years, American universities had almost no contact with mainland China. That changed quickly, however, following normalization of U.S.-China relations and the beginning of China's reform era. As the slow trickle of Chinese students coming to the United States became a steady flow, universities all over America began welcoming their first students from the People's Republic by the mid-1980s. A relatively small number of U.S. students and scholars also began to go to China for short-term study, and those American and Chinese universities with pre-1949 links sought to reinstate their connections.

George Mason University, founded in 1972, had no previous contacts with China on which to build in the 1980s. Nevertheless, its strong science programs and location in the metropolitan Washington D.C. region ensured that the school was not overlooked by Chinese graduate students coming to America. Some Chinese scholars retained links to the universities they had previously attended in China, helping to stimulate academic exchanges and research connections. Mason's links with the PRC grew naturally out of these student and faculty connections of the 1980s and 1990s. The university also began offering Chinese language courses in 1999 as well as a summer language program and other short-term programs in China a few years later.

Why Coordinate China Activities and How?

By 2003, when George Mason decided to hire a China coordinator, it had become one of the largest public universities in Virginia and was gaining a national reputation. Its proximity to Washington D.C. and its role as part of the booming high technology economy of Northern Virginia were key assets. It also had a thriving community of international students and scholars, many faculty members with international experience and research interests, and strong study abroad programs.

Given its already strong international orientation, what motivated the university to hire someone to coordinate China activities at this time? China came into focus as a priority at George Mason due to a combination of long-term goals and short-term opportunities.

First, for several years, university leaders had been thinking about taking a more strategic approach to internationalization. The university's global connections had been primarily defined by study abroad programs and exchanges initiated by the faculty. There had been little top-down institutional effort to promote international linkages. But, like other American universities, Mason had seen a drop in foreign student applications following September 11, 2001, and was wondering how to counter this trend. It was also interested in working on more ambitious academic programs with overseas universities. In a time of heightened international tension, America's higher education institutions were among the nation's most effective international ambassadors; George Mason and other universities were explicitly interested in finding ways to more effectively play this role.

Second, China appeared to have much to offer the university. Many Chinese university delegations had been coming to visit the Virginia campus and speaking enthusiastically about signing agreements and forming partnerships, vaguely defined, with American schools. At the same time, several Mason faculty members traveled to China and came back with tales of opportunity—Chinese entities eager to partner with Mason, including some that were even willing to offer land and buildings to form a branch campus of George Mason University in China.

These events were not unique to Mason—similar discussions were taking place on many American campuses at the time. But a third factor helped crystallize Mason's decision to take a more systematic approach to China. In 2002, then-Virginia Governor Mark Warner was planning a trip to Asia, and he asked George Mason and other public universities in Virginia to provide some background on their activities in the region. The provost asked Mason's different colleges and schools to list their Asia projects and the resulting compilation showed a preponderance of China activity—more than 60 China-related projects made the list—double the number of projects Mason had in India, Japan, Korea, and Vietnam combined. These projects were mainly small-scale initiatives such as research projects, exchanges of students and faculty, Memorandums of Understanding that were signed but not fully implemented, workshops, seminars, and training sessions. The School of Computational Sciences and the School of Public Policy, in particular, had developed good working relationships in China that seemed to have potential to grow.

This tantalizing and diverse list of China activities at Mason, combined with a growing sense of opportunity in China and the desire to raise the profile of the university's international activities, led the provost at George Mason to hire a part-time coordinator for China activities in 2003. This position was not meant to be a gatekeeper or to put the brakes on certain projects. Rather, the position would have two main functions—first, to support worthwhile existing activities on an as-needed basis and second, to help the university develop a strategy to guide new China-related initiatives on campus. Thus, the China administrator would hopefully bring one or two desirable new China-related projects to fruition, while still letting "a hundred flowers bloom" (and watering as necessary) at the department and faculty level.

The responsibilities of the China coordinator have evolved over time. The most immediate task was to learn about the ongoing China activities at Mason and play a supportive role. Gradually, as a China strategy took shape, new initiatives have absorbed a relatively large share of the coordinator's time. The China position is now full-time and the university has hired two new people to coordinate specific China projects as they grow in scope. In the following pages I will describe these dual aspects of coordinating China-related activities on campus and give examples of how this has worked in practice.

Efforts to Strengthen Existing Linkages

There was no lack of projects for the China coordinator to work on in 2003. Almost immediately there were requests for information and assistance from faculty and staff, delegations to be hosted, and many people to meet in order to better understand the needs on campus and the potential for new China initiatives. One of the coordinator's first projects was to review the university's previously signed agreements with institutions in the PRC to determine how many proposals were still current and what ongoing activities were involved. This was also a useful way to get updated on some of the university's past and present China activities. To give a sense of how a regional coordinator can contribute to a university's daily mix of activities, I will cite two examples—work with faculty going to China and work with delegations from China.

Work with faculty going to China

Mason faculty and staff travel to China for many reasons, such as to participate in conferences, give seminars, or teach short-term courses. From the beginning, some faculty members asked the China coordinator for assistance to make the most of such exchanges. For instance, in addition to their planned project or lectures, were there other people or institutions they should see? Did Mason have any institutional contacts or alumni in cities they planned to visit? Were there any university goals in China that they could advance by their visit?

One faculty member planned to stay in Shanghai for several months to do field research. He sought advice on how to locate think tanks and NGOs in China that might be interested in his work, where to find long-term reasonable housing, and how to make contact with potential research assistants and local guides in the city. Another faculty member planned to take a group of students to China to perform in an arts festival. After the festival, were there any universities in the area that they might visit? Would it make sense to stop in Hong Kong on the way out, and what

IIE/AIFS Foundation Global Education Research Reports
U.S.-China Educational Exchange: Perspectives on a Growing Partnership

75

institutions were involved in the arts there? Faculty members frequently seek this type of advice, research assistance, and networking suggestions.

Work with delegations from China

The China coordinator is also a logical first point of contact for delegations from China interested in visiting the campus. While some visitors are invited by a department or faculty member, others are seemingly cold calls from groups planning to visit the Washington D.C. area and wanting a better understanding of American higher education.

In the case of cold calls, the first step is to find out the primary purpose of a proposed visit, and determine who (if anyone) at Mason would be appropriate to meet the group. If that person is not able to meet the delegation, or if the delegation's interests do not mesh well with Mason's, the coordinator may suggest that the group visit other organizations instead.

For delegations with a clear and relevant purpose, it is usually not hard to find faculty and staff willing to meet with them and interested in sharing information. The coordinator can help by trying to think of different angles and bringing in other people to the meetings who may not have an obvious connection to the immediate topic but have something to contribute nonetheless. A delegation that wants to discuss a training program for nurses, for example, should meet not only with the Nursing School but also with a representative from the university's English Language Institute (since many Chinese trainees request some English language work) and with the Office of Continuing Professional Education, which administers most of these programs. In some cases, a Mason department may be eager to host a China delegation but need advice on how to present specific information, achieve certain goals or address protocol issues. In other cases, someone at the university may ask for help in following up on specific suggestions or projects resulting from a delegation visit.

The China coordinator usually takes primary responsibility for delegations that meet with the president or provost of the university or that plan to discuss topics of interest to the whole university. Finally, the coordinator keeps a list of delegations that have visited campus, including names of delegation members, major points of discussion, agreements signed if any, and recommended follow up. This list has proved very useful in maintaining continuity of contacts and as a reference point for many other China activities.

Setting Priorities and Encouraging New Programs

The second major role for the China coordinator has been to help identify worthwhile opportunities and to develop a coherent and sustainable approach to implementing them.

Given the number of unsolicited Chinese proposals that had been received on campus by 2003, the logical first step was to find out what type of international education ventures were meeting with success in China. This sobering survey of higher education projects in China showed a lot of well-intentioned agreements, but little concrete progress and many unanticipated roadblocks. China's Ministry of Education clearly played an active role in reviewing major education projects involving non-Chinese institutions and would not hesitate to shut down those that did not meet its criteria, though the criteria were not well defined. There were few rules and regulations governing Sino-foreign educational ventures. Those that existed made it clear that all foreign educational providers offering degree programs in China must do so with a Chinese partner.

Mason was ready to move up the ladder of international engagement with China. But given the relatively opaque operating environment and stumbling blocks encountered by so many projects, how could the university determine the best approach and the most appropriate Chinese partner for any such projects?

After exploring various options and assessing the level of interest and commitment in various departments on campus, two new initiatives, summarized briefly below, gradually emerged. These projects relied on the university's existing assets, did not seem likely to outpace our limited resources, and appeared to provide long-term benefits to the university. Both projects have moved forward, although not without twists and unanticipated turns.

The U.S.-China 1+2+1 Dual Degree Program

In 2004, George Mason became one of the first American universities to join the U.S.-China 1+2+1 Program. This program—an undergraduate dual degree program sponsored by the American Association of State Colleges and Universities (AASCU) and the China Council for International Education Exchange (CCIEE)—offered safeguards that seemed to reduce the risk of failure. The sponsors would provide valuable administrative support to participating universities in the U.S. and China, and the security of knowing that the project's goals were consistent with those of China's educational bureaucracy—the same bureaucracy making it difficult for many other U.S. projects to move off the drawing board. Of course, this approach also involves compromises because it requires participating universities to accept and play by rules that are not of their own making, and not always the methods they would have chosen on their own.

TABLE 6.1: GEORGE MASON'S PARTNER INSTITUTIONS IN THE U.S.-CHINA 1+2+1 PROGRAM (INCLUDES NUMBER OF STUDENTS FROM EACH SCHOOL, 2005-2008)

Nanjing Normal University	29
Wuhan University of Technology	29
Soochow University	17
Yunnan University	8
Shandong University at Weihai	7
Chongqing University	6
Southwest Jiaotong University	5
Beijing Normal University	2
Nanjing Univ. of Info. Science and Technology	2
Chang'an University	1
Communication University of China	1
Total	107

In the program, Chinese undergraduates spend their freshman year at a Chinese university, their sophomore and junior years at an American university and their senior year back at the original university in China. At the conclusion of the program, students receive baccalaureate degrees from both schools. From George Mason's perspective, the project had many attractions. It would enable Mason to develop close working relationships with several Chinese university partners. These partners could be selected by Mason with an eye to mutual compatibility from among a larger group of Chinese participating schools, most of them well-established and highly regarded provincial-level institutions. It would give Mason a pipeline of promising international undergraduates who were not otherwise likely to make their way to Mason. (Unlike graduate students, Chinese undergraduates have generally come to the U.S. in much smaller numbers due primarily to financial considerations and visa restrictions.) And, importantly, Mason could control the scope of the program and increase its involvement as it felt able to do so. For instance, Mason began by signing partnership agreements with five universities and accepting only a limited number of students in a handful of degree programs, later adding several partners, degree programs, and more students in line with Chinese demand and Mason capacity.

Because 1+2+1 students receive a tuition discount and come to the United States for just a portion of their undergraduate years, they are not "typical" students in many respects, and the program has required universities in China and the United States to develop appropriate procedures for this group. In addition to dedicated program staff (each participating university must have a full time 1+2+1 coordinator on campus) it has required a significant commitment from many campus offices, from Admissions to the Registrar and many others. It also requires a commitment from faculty—for example, Mason must work out detailed course plans with each partner school for the incoming students in each relevant degree program. This requires in-depth faculty interaction between partner universities and a detailed understanding of how Chinese institutions work. These course plans must meet the students' general education and departmental requirements at Mason as well as at their Chinese institution. They also involve careful faculty evaluations of dozens of courses on both sides to determine equivalencies and facilitate the transfer of credit in two directions.

This type of work has also helped Mason develop useful expertise. The university has gained experience running a dual-degree program without having to create the program from scratch, and many of the procedures developed for this program are transferable to other international programs. As Mason gets to know its Chinese partners better, it has found new areas of program interest with these schools outside of the 1+2+1 program. In short, it has helped to internationalize the university at a basic grassroots level, with practical applications to other situations. In just four years the program has grown to be George Mason's largest collaboration with China. And together with George Mason's establishment of a branch campus in the United Arab Emirates (which opened its doors in 2005), it is George Mason's largest international academic initiative to date.

The Chinese Language Licensure Program

Another important China initiative at George Mason University is the Chinese Language Licensure Program (CLLP), a preparation program for Chinese language teachers. The idea for this program grew out of discussions initiated by the College Board, which sought to encourage such training programs across the country in response to the rapidly growing demand for Chinese language classes in American elementary, middle, and high schools. The idea made sense for Mason because it was a logical extension of the university's existing Foreign Language Licensure Program (which originally offered Russian, Spanish, and other language tracks but not Chinese) as well as the university's own growing experience in teaching Chinese language.

The proposed CLLP would be housed in the university's College of Education and Human Development, but it would also rely significantly on faculty expertise in the university's Chinese language program, part of the College of Humanities and Social Science, as well as support from other parts of the university and the community. The China coordinator was able to help by bringing all the interested parties together to develop plans for the new program relatively quickly. In 2005, Mason received approval to offer this program and began to recruit its first class of students.

The China coordinator was able to play a supporting role in other ways as well. Soon after the licensure program began, George Mason University was contacted by the China Scholarship Council, which was interested in sending small groups of students from China to the CLLP for training and work experience in the United States. This exchange presented a relatively complex set of visa and other issues, but Mason and the CSC worked out the details and Mason began to receive cohorts of teachers from China each year beginning in fall 2007.

Finally, the new licensure program was of particular interest to nearby school systems, which were expanding their offerings of K-12 Chinese classes and eager to see the supply of certified Chinese teachers grow. Mason's China coordinator helped facilitate discussions with foreign language coordinators from nearby K-12 school systems and encouraged interactions between the university and the local schools. For example, a neighboring school system was interested in holding a Chinese language summer camp for elementary school students. The university was able to offer space for the camp, which in turn provided practical experience for the university's CLLP students and several camp counseling jobs for Mason's advanced Chinese language students, to the benefit of all the groups.

Looking Ahead

In the first week of September 2008, the *Mason Gazette* published two stories that illustrate the interlinking and continuing potential of the university's China connections.[1] On September 4, the *Gazette* published a story about the annual worldwide university rankings done by Shanghai Jiao Tong University's Institute of Higher Education. For the first time, Mason was ranked as one of the top 100 North and Latin American universities. The article quoted Mason's provost as saying that, "being recognized by Shanghai Jiao Tong University's Academic Ranking of World Universities is a very rewarding reflection of Mason's global outreach." The next day the *Gazette* carried a story about an assistant professor in Mason's Department of Molecular and Microbiology. Professor Wu, originally from China, led a research team that had just published a breakthrough study of how the HIV virus attacks cells in the immune system, which will undoubtedly bring more interest and recognition to the university in China and elsewhere.

More than five years after Mason hired a China coordinator, the university is more engaged with China than before 2003, and the level of activity continues to rise. Generalizing from my experience working on China-related activities at Mason, it would seem that, as the level of interactions in one region grows, so too do the ideas and opportunities for other projects in that region. As Mason gets to know its Chinese 1+2+1 university partners better and they send more students to our campus, the university sees other ways of working with these schools and will be better able to develop joint programs in different areas. As the Chinese Language Licensure Program trains more Chinese teachers, new opportunities emerge for Mason to network with local school districts and heritage Chinese schools. As the Chinese student and scholar community grows at Mason, the university may be able to offer more Chinese cultural programs of interest to the Mason community and beyond. And as more Mason graduates return to live and work in China, more Chinese alumni may be interested in maintaining contact with the university or helping current students studying in or about China.

This brief look at efforts to coordinate China exchanges on one campus necessarily simplifies some complex issues and gives only brief examples of a few activities and projects. Each university will have different needs and challenges, but anecdotally it seems that a regional approach to administering international activities may be useful on campuses with a sufficient level of activity, interest, and potential in a particular region. In the case of China, a growing number of universities have recently come by different routes to an interest in creating an office of China programs or designating a person to be responsible for administering varied China activities.

Given the high-profile success of the 2008 Summer Olympics in Beijing, there will almost certainly be another spike in the number of American students interested in learning about China and in exchange programs of various types. And China's continuing drive to internationalize its universities and make them word-class institutions makes it likely that there will continue to be Chinese schools eager to work with American counterparts for some time to come.

NOTE

[1] http://gazette.gmu.edu/archives.

Chaper Seven

The Language Flagship: Multiple Approaches to Creating Global Professionals

By Carl Falsgraf, University of Oregon

and Dana S. Bourgerie, Brigham Young University

Introduction: What is Flagship?

The Language Flagship, an initiative of the National Security Education Program (NSEP) in the U.S. Department of Defense, is a critical part of the National Security Language Initiative. Since its modest beginning in 2002 with four participating institutions, The Language Flagship has sought to produce global professionals in strategic languages with ACTFL Superior (ILR 3) language skills through a government-academic partnership.[1] In less than seven years, The Language Flagship has now grown to include twelve domestic Flagship centers, including three K-12 Flagship programs; seven overseas Flagship centers; and six Flagship partner programs, and three K-12 Flagship programs teaching African languages, Arabic, Chinese, Hindi/Urdu, Korean, Persian, Russian, and Central Asian Turkic languages. All focus on the upper range of the ACTFL and ILR proficiency scales with the aim of creating global professionals for government, business, industry, and education. In short, Flagship students do what thousands of overseas students do routinely in the United States. The Institute of International Education (IIE) administers this important program on behalf of NSEP by awarding and managing grants to Flagship institutions.

Although all Flagship programs have local contexts and language-specific challenges, they are tied together by a common set of principles and features. Each program is a part of The Language Flagship, which is committed to providing students with the linguistic and cultural skills necessary to become global professionals and to using an assessment system that includes standardized tests and portfolios. Most Flagship programs make use of domain language training, advanced cultural training, direct enrollment in target-country universities, and internships to help students achieve. Flagship programs do not limit recruitment to foreign language majors, but look for students with clear professional goals. At the heart of the Flagship movement is recognition that high linguistic proficiency alone is insufficient to meet the growing demands placed on professionals working in increasingly sophisticated international markets and government roles. Along with the linguistic proficiency goal of ACTFL Superior (ILR 3), students must develop cultural knowledge and specific domain knowledge to become true global professionals.

In a broader sense, The Language Flagship seeks to change the way languages are taught by infusing universities with a model of advanced learning to build capacity in critical languages and, eventually, all languages. Each Flagship pursues the mission to create global professionals by leveraging local resources, working within local constraints, and collaborating with local partners.

The Chinese Flagship Group

There are currently seven Chinese Flagship programs, each with somewhat different designations and charges:

- Brigham Young University Chinese Flagship Center (undergraduate/post-baccalaureate certificate)

- The University of Mississippi Chinese Flagship Center (undergraduate)

- The Ohio State University Chinese Flagship Center (K-16)

- The University of Oregon Chinese Flagship Center (K-16)

- Arizona State University Chinese Partner Program

- Indiana University Chinese Partner Program (2008)

- University of Rhode Island Chinese Partner Program (2008)

Two overseas centers serve the needs of all domestic Chinese programs:

- Nanjing University Chinese Flagship Center (BYU administered)

- Qingdao Chinese Flagship Center (OSU administered)

The domestic curricula of Flagship programs vary, though most operate as undergraduate programs. Among the Chinese programs, The Ohio State University Flagship program is the only one to offer both an undergraduate option and a master's degree. Brigham Young University's Flagship is an undergraduate program, but offers a certificate for a limited number of post-baccalaureate students. The University of Oregon operates as a four-year program, whereas Brigham Young University typically accepts students in the junior or senior year. Two of the Chinese centers (Ohio State University and the University of Oregon) are designated as K-16 centers charged with developing articulated K-16 models leading to superior proficiency.

Flagship programs all culminate in an overseas capstone, which includes direct enrollment at Nanjing University and internships managed by the Qingdao center. The overseas capstone experience in China requires students to negotiate Chinese academic and workplace culture, thus simulating their future roles as professionals working in Chinese-speaking contexts. Unlike traditional study abroad programs where students primarily enroll in protected courses designed for foreigners, the Nanjing Center facilitates enrollment in regular university courses matching students' domain interests or majors. They are also required to complete internships and/or community service in China to provide experiential learning opportunities.

This chapter will feature two successful Chinese Flagship programs at Brigham Young University (BYU) and the University of Oregon (UO), outlining the different ways that each pursues the common goal of creating global professionals.

The Brigham Young University Flagship Model

Institutional Context

In its seventh year of operation, the Brigham Young University Flagship Center is housed in and heavily integrated into the Department of Asian and Near Eastern Languages and affiliated with the university's Center for Language Studies (CLS). Both are units of the College of Humanities. The Department of Asian and Near Eastern Languages' Chinese program is among the largest in the U.S., with enrollments of around 1,500. The BYU Chinese program has seven full-time Chinese language faculty; three long-term, part-time instructors; and numerous student instructors. The Flagship Center benefits from support from other key campus units, including the Kennedy Center for International Studies, the International Study Programs Office, and the Global Management Center at the BYU Marriott School of Business.

Although Utah is not always associated with international activities or ethnic diversity, the area has significant minority populations, especially in the large population centers along the Wasatch Front where BYU is located.[2] The Salt Lake City area is also home to one of ten national refugee relocation centers in the United States. Utah's Asian population is around 2% (compared to 4% nationally). Despite the relatively low minority population in much of the state, Utah is rich with international experience. Over 60% of Utahans affiliate with the Church of Jesus Christ of Latter Day Saints (also referred to as Mormon or LDS), whose worldwide headquarters are located in Salt Lake City. The widespread tradition among young LDS church members to serve as volunteer missionaries throughout the world has contributed to a strong international interest in the state. BYU and other higher education institutions enroll large numbers of former missionaries with overseas residence and language experience. As a result, BYU has among the highest number of second language speakers in the nation, with more than 77% of the student body (85% of the seniors) speaking a second language.[3]

Recruitment and Admissions

Relating directly to its local context, the BYU Chinese Flagship Program draws heavily on students of BYU's large Chinese program, but also recruits nationally. Each year, about a fourth of the recruiting class comes from outside the university. Because of the strength of the Chinese program, the Flagship program admits students no earlier than the junior year, deferring early Chinese training to BYU's regular Chinese sections. In contrast to the Oregon Flagship Program, BYU's Flagship heritage population is small. Among the six cohorts (forty-two students) who have participated in the program, seven have been heritage learners and about half have been former missionaries from Chinese-speaking areas. The remainder of the students has been composed of learners who began studying in traditional courses. Most have had substantial experience with another foreign language and participated in traditional study abroad programs at least once. Recruitment for the undergraduate program comes mainly from freshmen and sophomores studying in the lower levels of the regular Chinese program.

Like other Flagship programs, BYU does not limit recruitment to Chinese majors. Many, but not all, recruits are double majors from a variety of fields. The program makes special efforts to approach college deans who are inclined to support international education and whose students have participated in the past. Majors have varied widely, but the most common have been accounting, business, economics, engineering, and international relations. Other fields have included journalism, microbiology, pre-med, and visual arts.

BYU has reached out to other state higher education institutions through its language and advising centers. The University of Utah and Utah State University represent good recruiting sources for the BYU program, since both have similar demographics. Nationally, BYU has used the networks of Chinese language associations to advertise its program. Applicants from the national pool are typically students seeking certificates as special status, post-baccalaureate students.

K-12 Partnerships and Program Articulation in Utah

As is the case throughout the U.S., Chinese language enrollments have burgeoned in Utah in the last five years. Although still a small percentage of the foreign language enrollments in Utah, the number of students studying Chinese has grown substantially from 183 in 2003 to 1,215 in 2007 (see Table 7.1 below), with a projected enrollment between 3,000-3,500 in 2008.

TABLE 7.1: CHINESE ENROLLMENTS IN UTAH FROM 2003 THROUGH 2007 (SECONDARY STUDENTS ONLY, GRADES 7-12)[4]

Language	Year									
	2003		2004		2005		2006		2007	
	Count	Pct	Count	Pct	Count	Pct	Count	Pct	Count	Pct
Chinese	183	0.25%	159	0.24%	263	0.39%	435	0.61%	1,215	1.54%
Total	73,983	100%	65,409	100%	68,258	100%	71,602	100%	78,878	100%

Source: Utah Department of Education, World Language Office

In 2003, fewer than six high school Chinese programs in Utah existed. In 2008, there will be seventy-four secondary school programs. Moreover, there will be ten Chinese dual language programs beginning in Utah for the 2009-10 school year in six different school districts (Alpine, Davis, Granite, Jordan, Provo, and Weber). Two more schools and school districts will join the immersion group in 2010-11 (Park City and Salt Lake City). Nearly all of this recent growth has been funded by bi-partisan legislation through two state bills:

- SB 80 (2007) Critical Language Program: $330,000 per year for six years for critical language programs in secondary schools.

- SB 41 (2008) Critical Language Program: $480,000 per year for six years for critical language programs in secondary schools and $280,000 for critical dual language programs in elementary schools (Chinese, French, Spanish) per year for six years.

These state-based incentives have taken much of the funding burden from the Flagship Center and allowed it to focus on curriculum support, materials development, assessment support, and teacher training.

The BYU Flagship has used existing funds and recently allocated K-12 linkage funds to respond to specific requests from the World Languages Unit at the Utah Department of Education and from individual districts. Two BYU Flagship Center-sponsored efforts are the Chinese EDNET distance program for high schools and a STARTALK Program (http://startalk.umd.edu), which includes both a K-12 intensive Chinese language camp and an associated teacher training workshop. Initiated in 2007 and administered by the University of Maryland's National Foreign Language Center, STARTALK is a part of a nationwide, federally funded effort to support critical language study in the U.S.

Now in its second year, EDNET (http://ednet.byu.edu) serves twenty-five high schools. The main course originates from the BYU campus and from the Granite School District in the Salt Lake City area and is transmitted through a video linkup provided by the Utah Education Network. An experienced master teacher leads these live and interactive broadcasts, which are recorded for occasional delayed broadcast. Each classroom has a Chinese-speaking facilitator on-site to support the live lesson and to carry out specifically designed activities.

The STARTALK program plays two distinct roles in the BYU Flagship K-12 strategy. STARTALK exposes more students to Chinese earlier and helps bolster high school enrollments through its articulated curriculum. In addition, the program serves as an important recruitment tool for the Flagship program as STARTALK students connect with advanced students, who serve as counselors.

The 2008 STARTALK workshop served eighteen secondary teachers and perspective teachers, along with fifteen teachers from China's Hanban (National Office for Teaching Chinese as a Foreign Language). This ongoing workshop series helps address the critical need for qualified teachers by providing a methods course toward alternative certification. Partly as a result of the teacher workshop, the Brigham Young University Chinese Flagship program sponsors a Utah Chinese language teachers association, which was formally organized in September 2008.

In addition to EDNET and STARTALK, the BYU Flagship is working with the university's independent study unit to develop a model course for Chinese. Each of these three efforts are articulated and coordinated in terms of curriculum and credit with regular Chinese programs in Utah, allowing students to move smoothly from one program to another. Thus, the relationship between the state and the BYU Flagship represents a true partnership, and each works together in a complementary fashion toward larger state goals.

The BYU Advanced Program: Structure and Pedagogical Approach

As with the other Flagship programs, the BYU program strives to produce graduates capable of performing professionally in the target language. Although BYU begins to recruit students in their freshman year and, increasingly, in the K-12 sector, the BYU program does not formally admit students until at least the junior year. The BYU Flagship approaches the lower-division training with the goal of helping to build capacity and then to draw from that strengthened applicant pool for formal admission into the program. After admission, the pedagogical focus shifts to domain specific and content-based work, correlating directly with students' professional area of focus. Table 7.2 describes the tracks available to participants in the BYU Flagship program, and Table 7.3 shows details of these tracks.

TABLE 7.2: BYU CHINESE FLAGSHIP TRACK DESCRIPTIONS

Track	Duration	Description
Junior Track	3 Years	For Intermediate/Intermediate-High students who still need to complete substantial major work and upper-level general Chinese training (e.g., media Chinese, literary Chinese, and literature survey). Restricted to matriculating BYU students.
Senior Track	2 Years	For students who have largely completed their majors and who can devote most of their time to Flagship-specific study. For registered BYU students (current or transfer students).
Fast Track	1 Year	For candidates entering at a minimum of ACTFL Advanced (ILR 2+/3) and who have already completed upper-level cultural and linguistic training. Ideal for at-large candidates who have done other substantial study outside of BYU.

TABLE 7.3: Available Tracks for the BYU Flagship Program

Academic Year		Sep Oct Nov Dec	Jan Feb Mar Apr	May Jun Jul Aug
JUNIOR TRACK	Y1	Advanced Chinese Major course work Specialty advisement	Advanced Chinese Major course work Specialty advisement	Optional Flagship Major courses
	Y2	Domain and content training	Domain and content training	
	Y3 Overseas	Direct enrollment in Nanjing	Internship in China	
SENIOR TRACK/ Special status post-BA	Y1	Domain and content training	Domain and content training Culture course	Domain and content training
	Y2 Overseas	Direct enrollment in Nanjing	Internship in China	
FAST TRACK (1 Year)		Domain and content training	Direct enrollment in Nanjing Culture course	Internship in China

The BYU program is not only designed for flexibility in terms of entry point but also for accommodating the great variability in student background that is typical of high-level language training. BYU Flagship's curriculum is among the most individualized of all the Flagship programs. The core of the special purpose coursework is organized around a set of tutorials. Students are expected to learn independently, and the domain training consists of one-on-one tutorials and small group work. The overall scheme is outlined in Table 7.4 below.

TABLE 7.4: Description of Flagship Coursework

Course or Activity	Hours per Week	Description
Domain Tutorials	2	One-on-one work with dedicated Flagship instructors and graduate assistants according to specialized, domain-based curriculum plan
Domain Tutorial (small group)	1	Students present ongoing research and work to classmates and teachers
Advanced Rhetorical Skills	2	Advanced rhetorical skills such as debate, argument, and use of proper language registers
Peer Domain Tutor Sessions	5	Regular work with native tutors chosen to match students' major interests
Hybrid Content Courses (similar to Languages Across the Curriculum)	Variable	Target language recitation sections attached to key English content courses such as Chinese political science, Chinese history
Supplemental Chinese Courses	Variable	Courses in modern literature, literary Chinese, media Chinese as needed

The individualized nature of the BYU Chinese Flagship program accommodates a large number of domain interests. However, the instructors are not necessarily specialists in the students' domain areas, and they do not have access to the specialist-led content courses that exist in some programs. BYU mitigates this disadvantage by relying extensively on native graduate student tutors who are trained to help students learn about the specialty language and practice of their common field of interest. BYU-CFP also makes use of target language content recitations attached to selected regular courses, which is similar to the Languages Across the Curriculum approach.

Different Paths to China

All Chinese Flagship programs design their programs with the two components of the overseas capstone experience in mind: Direct enrollment at the BYU-managed Flagship Center at Nanjing University and internship placement through the Qingdao Flagship Center. The domestic domain and cultural training prepares students for direct enrollment in their major courses at Nanjing University and then to complete an internship with a company or institution in China. The direct enrollment phase allows students to study alongside native classmates, which is common in the U.S. but rare for American students in China. Students have a chance to live with a native-speaking roommate with a similar academic background. Thus, students gain experience by studying in a Chinese context and establishing collegial relationships with future Chinese professionals.

Students typically complete internships after the direct enrollment phase. The Ohio State University-managed Qingdao Flagship Center places Flagship students in internships. When possible, the interns are placed in native institutions to allow for maximum exposure to Chinese professional practices.

Assessment and Evaluation

The National Security Education Program, which funds The Language Flagship, has insisted on accountability, and the BYU Chinese Flagship program uses a number of assessment and evaluation tools. ACTFL-OPI, the Chinese government HSK, and two computer adaptive tests for listening and reading[5] form the core of the standardized measures for the BYU program. BYU also has made use of the Standards-based Measurement of Proficiency (STAMP) developed by the Center for Applied Second Language Studies (CASLS), the parent unit of the University of Oregon Flagship program. When available, BYU has used the Defense Language Proficiency Test (DLPT), one of the Interagency Language Roundtable (ILR) assessment tools.

In addition to the various standardized measures, the BYU Chinese Flagship program collects qualitative data through program surveys, learning journals, and internship providers' surveys. To better serve the Flagship community and the language field as a whole, BYU collects both qualitative data and proficiency tests scores for research and formative evaluation.

Moreover, because there is much that cannot be captured in a standardized test, BYU makes use of language portfolios to display the outcomes of the students' efforts, including student presentations, writing samples, resumes, and linguistic history.

Collaboration and Cooperation

Although Flagship models vary, each program works toward producing professionals who have the linguistic and cultural ability to conduct business in Chinese. A key attribute of the Flagship movement is that each program is part of a larger network that draws upon expertise of its language group and of other Flagship language programs. For example, overseas centers serve all programs, and designated K-16 centers such as Ohio State University and the University of Oregon have developed curricula and expertise for Chinese K-12 programs, which can be shared with other emerging programs in Utah and elsewhere. Moreover, programs share assessment tools and portfolio systems.

Oregon Chinese Flagship

The Oregon Context

The University of Oregon (UO), like BYU and other Flagships, works toward creating global professionals and changing the way languages are taught in the United States. The demographic, institutional, and historical context in which the UO works, however, has led to specific program choices related to design and focus that differ from program choices at BYU. As a Pacific Rim state in which 60% of economic activity involves overseas trade, Oregon has a large population of heritage Chinese speakers, and most have a strong individual motivation to master Chinese and other Asian languages. A tradition of ambivalence toward public education and recent tax cuts, however, has left public schools and universities under funded and unable to provide consistent access to quality language education. Nevertheless, local control has allowed a few oases of excellence to spring up. For example, Portland Public Schools (PPS) offers ten high-quality immersion programs in Chinese, Spanish, and Japanese. Most of these were established in response to community campaigns for specific schools and languages, but immersion has now become a cornerstone of the district's strategy to attract students who otherwise might attend suburban or private schools. Similarly, the University of Oregon has not generally distinguished itself as a national leader in language education, but decentralized administration and support for entrepreneurial activities has allowed the Center for Applied Second Language Studies (CASLS), a research and development center unaffiliated with any academic department, to flourish and gain a national reputation for innovation in language assessment, professional development, and technology. Furthermore, a large number of UO faculty and graduate students are native speakers of Mandarin Chinese, providing a rich environment for language learning across campus.

Approach and Philosophy

The approach and philosophy of the Oregon Chinese Flagship result directly from these special local conditions. The presence of a large and vibrant heritage community led to a strategic decision to focus initially on heritage speakers. The excellence of the PPS Chinese immersion program will lend itself to a long-term strategy of articulating that program with the UO Flagship to ensure a mix of heritage and non-heritage students. In addition, the many Chinese-speaking faculty across academic departments at UO were seen as a valuable potential resource for the program, which led the Flagship to bring content to the forefront of language learning in order to leverage these faculty resources to greatest effect.

This general approach dovetailed with NSEP's request for an articulated K-16 approach to developing ACTFL Superior (ILR 3) speakers of Mandarin Chinese through a close collaboration between an institution of higher education and a K-12 school system. The wisdom behind the NSEP approach is clear: few who begin language study after the age of eighteen achieve native-like phonological, syntactic, and pragmatic accuracy. Clearly, the long-term answer to America's language needs is to provide intensive and extended learning sequences starting at a young age. Portland Public Schools, with a history of excellence in immersion education and highly successful Chinese immersion and heritage programs, is an ideal site to develop and verify such a model. Furthermore, a long and close relationship between PPS and CASLS ensured that the inevitable difficulties and challenges of such an ambitious program would be dealt with in an atmosphere of trust and mutual understanding. The undergraduate experience at the UO leveraged campus strengths in language assessment and the university's large number of Chinese-speaking faculty.

At all levels, the Oregon Chinese Flagship rests on three basic principles:

- Content-based learning
- Explicit instruction
- Experiential learning

Although the nature of these experiences varies according to students' ages, students at all levels learn content through the language, develop metalinguistic awareness, and learn outside the formal classroom.

Creating Global Professionals

This approach to language and culture learning derives directly from the Flagship mandate to create global professionals. Effective global professionals must, of course, have excellent language and culture skills. In addition, they must possess critical thinking skills and master a professional or academic domain. From kindergarten through college, therefore, Oregon Chinese Flagship students learn age-appropriate content in Chinese, providing them with the lexis, conventions, and sociocultural norms associated with various domains. An elementary school student, for example, would be exposed to vocabulary such as "photosynthesis" and "cell nucleus," learn the conventions of writing a lab report in Chinese in high school and college, and then be initiated into the sociocultural norms of the field by interning in a Chinese biology lab. Such a student would presumably reach the ACTFL Superior (ILR 3) level on a general proficiency test and have the specialized skills and abilities within the biology domain to succeed in a Chinese-speaking environment.

Portland Public Schools' Chinese Flagship Program

Extraordinary individuals in extraordinary programs can achieve the remarkable result of Superior language and culture skills in a four-year college experience. Producing large numbers of global professionals, however, requires high-quality K-12 programs closely articulated with collegiate programs. Because the Oregon Chinese Flagship hinges on undergraduates enrolling in college-level classes in Chinese, incoming freshman need to have Advanced-level language skills. The two reliable ways to develop such skills are language immersion and heritage language programs. Portland Public Schools (PPS), nationally known for excellence in both areas, serves as the ideal laboratory for developing and verifying such a model.

PPS established the Mandarin Immersion Program at Woodstock Elementary in 1998. This program follows the basic tenets of partial immersion:

- At least half the day is spent in the target language.

- Classes follow the regular PPS curriculum.

- The target language is the medium of instruction.

The Mandarin Immersion Program diverges from past immersion orthodoxy by explicitly teaching the language, in some aspects. The approach, however, mirrors language arts instruction in English, not the abstract explications of grammar common in traditional high school and college foreign language classes. The aim of direct engagement with the language is to develop metalinguistic awareness and to engage learners' higher thinking skills, not to train specialists in syntax.

Now in its tenth year, The Mandarin Immersion Program will begin graduating students in 2011. Until then, verifying whether the articulation between K-12 and university is as smooth as planned will be impossible. Initial results from the UO program, however, are already informing and shaping instruction at the K-12 level, raising the odds that significant numbers of students will be prepared to handle college-level work in Chinese by the time they graduate.

Since becoming part of the Oregon Chinese Flagship in 2005, the PPS Mandarin Immersion Program has focused efforts in curriculum and professional development. While the content is determined by state and local curricula, immersion schools commonly fail to plan for language acquisition. Early claims that immersion students could acquire full proficiency by intense and prolonged exposure to the target language have not been borne out. As a result, PPS created a language curriculum for Japanese immersion based on forms, functions, and topics that students need to master at each grade level. This model, applied to Chinese, ensures that children progress in their linguistic development, and does not assume that getting by in academic courses is prima facie evidence of language acquisition.

The development of this curriculum has proven to be the perfect centerpiece for professional development as well. Instead of simply telling teachers what to do, instructional leaders and outside consultants have facilitated language curriculum development projects and used these as a platform for introducing research, techniques, and pedagogic principles. This "learn-by-doing" approach is an effective means of transmitting knowledge as well as a model of the many strategies teachers can use in their classrooms.

The Student Population

The original NSEP request for proposals called for a "K-16 pipeline" through which students could move smoothly from kindergarten through university. The reality is much more complex, but also more exciting and sustainable than the original pipeline model. Students rarely travel a straight pipeline path. Heritage learners in particular follow widely divergent and idiosyncratic paths to proficiency. Many build on basic oral skills acquired at home by attending private weekend schools to develop literacy skills.

In Portland, the heritage population consists predominantly of Cantonese speakers. Calling a Cantonese speaker a heritage speaker of Mandarin is somewhat like calling a Spanish speaker a heritage speaker of French. Although Cantonese speakers generally identify themselves culturally and ethnically as "Chinese," the two languages have very different phonological and syntactic features that make them mutually unintelligible. Most UO Flagship scholars have been in the U.S. at least since elementary school, all have been in the U.S. at least four years, and a significant number are American-born Chinese (ABC). In addition, a number of non-heritage students are reaching Intermediate proficiency through a variety of traditional and non-traditional means. As at BYU, most are recruited on campus and have lived in China and had some formal instruction.

TABLE 7.5: CURRENT COMPOSITION OF UNIVERSITY OF OREGON FLAGSHIP STUDENTS

Non-heritage	41%
Mandarin heritage	14%
Cantonese heritage	24%
American-born Chinese (Chinese-American)	22%

Underclassmen: Preparing for the Overseas Capstone

The true measure of being a global professional, at UO and other Chinese Flagship programs, is the ability to function effectively in a Chinese-speaking environment.

For undergraduates, this goal necessitates enrolling in academic classes at a Chinese university with native-speaking Chinese students and participating in an internship related to their academic or professional interests.

UO Flagship Scholars prepare for this experience during their freshman and sophomore years in three ways: 1) taking regular university content courses in Chinese, 2) receiving specialized language instruction tied to those content courses, and 3) living in a Chinese-speaking environment.

UO Flagship Scholars generally take one regular college course each term in Chinese. Recent course offerings include Chinese Film, Green Chemistry, Modern Chinese History, and China's Urban Transformation. These courses are taught exclusively in Chinese, including lectures, readings, class discussions, papers, and tests. A customized language strategies course accompanies each class to provide linguistic support for the content course and to develop students' overall language proficiency. For example, the language strategies class tied to the China's Urban Transformation course introduces key vocabulary and discourse types associated with urban planning to help students comprehend lectures and readings. Students in the language strategies class might give a presentation, write an essay, or conduct a debate on the content topic to utilize the new academic and linguistic skills they have acquired. In addition, during their sophomore year, Flagship Scholars begin formulating topics and research strategies for writing a senior honors thesis entirely in Chinese using primary and secondary Chinese sources. This combination of rigorous academic work accompanied by language instruction follows the fundamental Oregon Chinese Flagship principles of content-based learning and explicit instruction.

An immersive living environment created for Flagship Scholars embodies the third fundamental principle, experiential learning. Flagship scholars live in a special wing of an international dorm with a native speaker of Chinese as resident advisor. A variety of activities, including dinners, guest lectures, and films conducted in Chinese, help create a Chinese-speaking environment within the confines of the university.

The Junior Year Overseas Capstone Experience

Each Flagship institution has significant latitude in determining the program model and pedagogic approach, yet all share a commitment to an extended overseas academic and internship experience. This capstone experience is a "dress rehearsal" for being a true global professional. The Oregon Chinese Flagship places more emphasis on the academic aspects of the experience to ensure a strong foundation in a major discipline and to ensure that reasonably diligent students graduate in four years.

University of Oregon (UO) courses are mostly general education classes, so Flagship Scholars are encouraged to take courses in their major areas at Nanjing University's Flagship China Center. In this way, every student has a solid basis in wide range of liberal arts topics in Chinese as well as deep knowledge of their area of specialization. Flagship Scholars spend their entire academic year in Nanjing. During spring term, they participate in community service projects related to their areas of interest. They also are encouraged to gather information and conduct research in preparation for writing their theses during their senior years.

The Senior Honors Thesis

Upon returning from Nanjing University, Flagship Scholars begin writing a senior honors thesis in Chinese. Two faculty advisors, one a domain specialist and one a language specialist, will assist students in this endeavor. The standards for this thesis will be roughly equivalent to those for students in the UO Honors College who write honors theses in English.

Conclusion

The Chinese Flagship programs at Brigham Young University and the University of Oregon share common goals and philosophies. Both are focused on creating global professionals, which requires ACTFL Superior (ILR 3) proficiency in the language as well as expertise in a particular domain and the ability to work effectively in a Chinese cultural context. The two programs require students to spend a year in China taking classes at Nanjing University and participating in internships. A wide array of assessment methods, including standardized tests and portfolios, determines success. Individual students and the programs themselves are held accountable for results on these measures. Finally, both programs work closely with K-12 programs in the firm belief that early and sustained language programs are the long-term solution to the nation's language needs.

The institutional, political, and demographic contexts in which these programs operate, however, are quite different. The excellent Chinese language program and large contingent of returning missionaries at BYU provide a supply of students on campus and nearby from which to recruit. Oregon, on the other hand, is home to a large heritage population. Thus, 83% of BYU Flagship students are non-heritage, compared with 41% of Oregon students. A large and diverse Chinese-speaking faculty at Oregon provides an ideal environment for a "languages across the curriculum" approach in which underclassmen take general education classes in Chinese. Because BYU only accepts upperclassmen, however, a more individualized approach allows for specialized, domain- specific instruction. While still young, both programs appear to be successful in developing the linguistic, cultural, academic, and professional skills required of a global professional.

This paper has described how two very different institutions pursue a common educational goal by very different means. These models can inform the efforts of other institutions seeking to become Flagship Partners and provide their students with similar opportunities.

NOTES

[1] American Council on the Teaching of Foreign Languages (ACTFL) Proficiency Assessments are developed in accordance with the published ACTFL Proficiency Guidelines, a national metric for measuring language competence based on the U.S. government's Interagency Language Roundtable (ILR) language descriptors, and adapted for applicability in an academic setting. For information on specific criteria for Superior-level speaking, reading, listening and writing proficiency, please visit: https://www.languagetesting.com/assessments_academic.cfm.

[2] The 2006 census (http://quickfacts.census.gov/qfd/states/41000.html) places Salt Lake City's Hispanic population at 18.8%, more than the national average of 14.8%. In addition, the Pacific Islander population is just under 2%, African American 1.9%, and Native American 1.3%.

[3] Brigham Young University's Center for Language Studies.

[4] These numbers are based on October 1 course enrollment data for each academic year.

[5] Computer-Adaptive Test for Reading Chinese (CATRC), Chinese Computerized Adaptive Listening Comprehension Test (CCALT), and *Hanyu Shuiping Kaoshi* (HSK).

Chapter Eight

WORKING WITH U.S. HIGHER EDUCATION: A CHINESE PERSPECTIVE

BY WANG YINGJIE, BEIJING NORMAL UNIVERSITY

This year is the 30th anniversary of China's implementation of the policy of Reform and Opening Up, and sending students abroad should be regarded as a reflection of that policy in the area of higher education. Deng Xiaoping, the general architect of the policy, said on June 23, 1978,

> I would like to see more students sent abroad. They should mainly study science, and should be sent by thousands instead of dozens. ...This is a better way to promote science and education for China. Now our progress is too slow; we need to send more students faster and broaden our methods of sending. On the one hand, we must strive to raise the level of our own universities, and on the other, we must send students abroad. Then we can have a comparison to see how good our universities really are.

His instruction was made reality before the end of the year. Since then waves of students and scholars have followed in the steps of the first delegations.

Today, ambitious young people want a world-class education. Educational collaboration is preparing young people to become leaders for the 21st century. Acquiring an international perspective is critical in today's fast paced and rapidly developing inter-dependent world. In the era of globalization, cross-cultural experience and an international perspective are vital for an individual to have full personal realization and for a nation to achieve competitiveness. In this sense, to study abroad is a key to unlocking the door to individual and national prosperity. More and more young people are going abroad to study, and the government, higher education institutions, and individuals have taken the initiative to find ways to support study abroad.

I was one of those ambitious young people anxious to see a world beyond China in the early 1980s. I was lucky enough to receive the opportunity to study abroad after passing a very competitive examination, and went to the U.S. to study at Stanford University from 1980 to 1982. I have benefited from this experience throughout my professional career. After I came back to my institution, Beijing Normal University, I was appointed dean and vice-president responsible for international cooperation and exchange. Now I conduct comparative study on Chinese and American higher education as a chair professor at Beijing Normal University.

Impact on Chinese Universities

The Chinese higher education system has undergone tremendous change since 1978. The era of higher education reforms coincided with a period of high numbers of students going abroad. Many returnees work at universities, and assume leading positions in university administration or become leading authorities in their own fields of study. A survey by the Ministry of Education in 2001 found that 51 percent of presidents of the state universities under the Ministry of Education have studied abroad. Eighty percent of the members of Chinese Academy of Sciences and Chinese Academy of Engineering who work in these state universities have experience abroad, as do 90 percent of deans. The returnees are one of the major driving forces of reforms in Chinese higher education.

First, the returnees brought back new ideas about what a university should be. After they came back, they spread the idea that the university is a place where the truth is pursued, transmitted and applied. They felt after their studies abroad that each member of the university community should simultaneously conduct research, teach and serve society. They adopted the American research university as an ideal model for university organization. They wanted the transformation of Chinese universities to reflect the following characteristics of the American research university:

- American research universities are national centers for basic research. The university budget for basic research mainly comes from federal agencies. Most of the national laboratories are on university campuses, and the government depends on research universities to meet challenges in defense, space exploration, public health, environmental protection, production efficiency, and social well-being, among other fields.

- American research universities are "multiversities." Research universities offer many subjects, sometimes including hundreds of programs, tens of thousands of students, and thousands of professors and staff. The research universities assume three missions: teaching, research and service.

- American research universities emphasize graduate education and professional education over undergraduate education, though they have tried to balance their focus in recent years.

- American universities are decentralized. Typically, a board of trustees governs the university, the president is appointed by the board to manage the daily operations of the university, and the faculty is responsible for academic affairs. Power is also distributed among three layers of administration: department, college and university. American research universities, in general, respect and guard the principle of the "three A's": academic autonomy, academic freedom and academic neutrality.

Taking my university, Beijing Normal University (BNU) as an example, one can see how much Chinese universities have adapted to emulate the American research university model. BNU has been one of China's best universities throughout its history, but before the 1980s, its mission had been mainly to train secondary school teachers. It was fairly small and had less than five thousand undergraduate students. Research was not considered a major mission at BNU, or at other universities in China.

Today, "publish or perish" is a very real phenomenon on campus. BNU has twenty research institutes and centers. Between 2001 and 2005, BNU faculty won 731 research grants in humanities and social sciences, and 625 research grants in science and technology from government agencies. From 2001 to 2006, faculty members and graduate students published 3,476 articles in journals listed by three major international academic journal indexes (SCI, EI and ISTP).

BNU began to enroll graduate students in 1978, when China resumed graduate education after cancelling it completely during the Cultural Revolution. China adopted the degree system in 1981, which was basically modeled on the Anglo-American system, and BNU granted its first master's degrees in 1981. Now, graduate students make up half of all full-time students at BNU, and the university granted 534 doctoral degrees in the 2007/2008 academic year. The Ministry of Education and the university authorities have made special policies to require and encourage faculty members to teach undergraduate courses. In the 1980s, the university only had a dozen departments dedicated to traditional humanities, social science and natural science fields, but now it has twenty-four colleges and schools covering many fields of study, including humanities, social sciences, education, law, management, business, sciences, engineering, medicine, and agriculture, and even a program of national defense. It enrolled 19,543 full-time students in the 2007/2008 school year, including 8,529 undergraduate students, 8,999 graduate students, and 2,015 international students registered in its long-term programs, which last a minimum of one semester. It also enrolls more than 10,000 students in its extension and online programs.

In the 1980s, not many people in China considered questions of balance of power in the academy, even within the walls of the universities. But today, Beijing Normal University has the Academic Council and the Academic Degree Committee, which make decisions and recommendations on academic issues. Academic autonomy and academic freedom are hot topics on campus and attract the interest of researchers in higher education. From all the developments described above, we can conclude that if the top Chinese universities are not copying the model of American research universities, they have definitely learned from it.

While Chinese universities have gained many advantages by adopting the American research university as a model, they also have begun to face some of the problems of large research universities. When "publish or perish" becomes a guiding principle and graduate education occupies the center of the university, undergraduate education may suffer. As the university becomes a multiversity, administrative bureaucracy may grow in influence at the expense of academic autonomy. If the university grows too much, it may find it difficult to serve the individual needs of faculty and students, who too easily become numbers instead of living persons from the perspective of the administration.

In light of all these problems, there is one big question that we need to think about: Can or should all Chinese universities follow the American research university model? To answer this question, Dr. Kathryn Mohrman wrote:

> It was a reflection to me of the danger expressed by Philip Altbach and others that we are developing only one model of higher education worldwide—a western, perhaps predominantly American model. The combined impact of the WTO, World Bank loans for higher education, and the dominance of the west on developing countries all have pushed China and other nonwestern nations to emulate their more affluent and prestigious brethren. It's a form of intellectual colonialism that some commentators find dangerous. In my opinion, it perpetuates a kind of inferiority complex among Chinese academics that seems unhealthy to me.[1]

In addition to bringing back ideas about the organizational structure of the university, returnees also promoted curriculum and instructional reforms based on their experience abroad. The university is a product of cultural heritage. In Chinese cultural traditions, teachers are supposed to take a role in the students' life "just next to heaven, earth, emperor and father," and therefore teachers are put in the center of the learning process. To learn knowledge by heart is essential for students to pass examinations, which are the culmination of the students' education. Teachers dominate the classroom and students take notes all the time. To respect students' choices and initiatives is something unknown to some teachers. This tradition was strengthened when we followed the model of the Soviet Union. We emphasized specialized education, neglecting the breadth of undergraduate education in the process. We paid too much attention to standardized requirements for all students, neglecting the development of individual character. We emphasized knowledge transmission, neglecting to train students in problem-solving. These paradigms dominated campus life in Chinese universities up to the mid-1980s.

The returnees had a very different educational experience in American universities. They had to be responsible for their own learning, and to exercise freedom in selecting majors and courses. They learned not only facts and specific knowledge, but also the ability to think critically, from which they benefitted for the rest of their lives. When they returned, they felt China had to have reforms in curriculum and instruction to prepare professionals with competencies to work in the fast changing world.

The first reform they promoted, beginning in the mid-1980s, was to adopt the system of credit units. All courses offered in Chinese universities had been required, and students had not had any choice of elective courses before the reform. With this system now implemented, students have greater choice of in courses, professors and scheduling. Students also gain a certain power in faculty evaluation: they can either evaluate "by their feet" walking into or out of the courses, or formally complete evaluation forms when the courses end.

WORKING WITH U.S. HIGHER EDUCATION: A CHINESE PERSPECTIVE

The second reform was to introduce general education (we sometimes call it *wenhua suzhi jiaoyu*, which literally means "cultural quality education") in the undergraduate curriculum. When we followed the Soviet model in the 1950s, we developed a very specialized academic program. Our students in fact began to study their area of specialization as soon as they entered the university, and took about 90 percent of their courses within their own departments. Since the introduction of the general education reform, all students must fulfill distribution requirements, including courses in areas such as humanities, social sciences, sciences, mathematics, technology, arts, sustainable development, and physical education.

The third reform has not been officially promoted at a nationwide level, but has a definite impact throughout the nation's campuses. The returnees have tried new teaching methods which they learned from their studies in the U. S., including offering seminar courses stressing interaction with students, welcoming or at least allowing students to challenge them in their classrooms, and experimenting with new forms of assessment, including thesis writing, oral examinations, and pass or fail grades.

Let's take BNU as an example again. BNU adopted the credit units system in the mid-1980s, and today undergraduates have to complete 155 to 165 units in order to graduate, including major and general education requirements. The actual number of credit requirements varies depending on the area of study. Elective courses make up about 20-30 percent of total required credit units for graduation. Three major curricular reforms took place in 1993, 1998 and 2003, and the university is currently reviewing its undergraduate curriculum again, so curricular reform has taken place regularly every five years.

The students' learning experience has been greatly expanded through these reforms. They can now select a second major or a minor. Their general education program consists mainly of eight sections, which are political science and moral education (16 units), foreign languages (10 units), computing technology (6 units), physical education and health (5 units), arts (2 units), military education (2 units), interdisciplinary presentations in humanities, social sciences, natural sciences, life sciences (4 units), and free elective courses (8-12 units). The general education program represents about one third of undergraduate course requirements for graduation. BNU has held Liyun Experimental Classes, in which students have an even broader educational experience, and they can postpone their selection of their major to the end of their sophomore year. BNU also offers an honors program for outstanding students. Students selected by this program can register in advanced graduate courses and be admitted to university graduate programs without taking the national graduate entrance examination, as long as they have done well in their courses. Student evaluation of instructors constitutes an important part of faculty assessment.

Generally speaking, students at BNU now are more responsible for their own learning, have more freedom of course selection, and have more opportunity to pursue an education that is both broad and specialized.

New Trends in Higher Education Exchanges

Four new trends have emerged in recent years, which together provide a dynamic picture of growth in educational exchange between China and the rest of the world. The first new trend is that China attracts more and more international students, including quite a few students registered in degree programs. This trend is obvious at BNU, which enrolled 1,881 short and long-duration international students in 2001, and 2,886 in 2005. While most international students are from Asia, Chinese campuses also host large numbers of European and American students. The government summarizes its policy objectives in the area of educational exchange as "enlarging enrollment, raising education level, assuring quality, and rationalizing management,"[2] and Chinese universities have reacted very positively to this policy. For Chinese universities, there are practical reasons to increase international student enrollment. Having more international students indicates that a university has begun to achieve world-class status, and international students provide a good and reliable source of revenue. In the era of reduced national funding for institutions, it is especially important for universities to have access to funds that they can use freely without excessive government control.

The second trend is that Chinese college students have more chances to study abroad. When Chinese universities signed exchange agreements with overseas universities in the past, Chinese students were usually not involved in exchange. But today, with students and universities in a better financial position than in the past, more Chinese students have started to benefit from exchange agreements. An exchange program at BNU in 2001 sent only 4 students abroad, but 41 of our students were sent abroad on exchange programs in 2006. The College of Economics at BNU sends a dozen students abroad for field work each year. Students at the School of Education now compete for the chance to attend international conferences abroad.

The third trend is that Chinese language programs have been greatly expanded. The Chinese government has promoted Chinese language learning throughout the world in recent years. By 2001, the government had opened 40 HSK (Chinese Proficiency Test) testing sites in 27 Chinese cities and 55 testing sites abroad, and the test had been taken by over 350,000 people from 120 countries. The government has also sponsored the establishment of Confucius Institutes, which are centers for promotion of Chinese language learning. The government policy on Confucius Institutes is very flexible: "A Confucius Institute can be established in various ways, with the flexibility to respond to the specific circumstances and requirements found in different countries. Any legal person or corporate body capable of facilitating language instruction and conducting educational and cultural exchange activities is eligible to apply for permission to establish a Confucius Institute." According to the Office of Chinese Language Council International (Hanban), as of March 2008 there were 238 Confucius Institutes (classes) in 69 countries and regions, since the first one was established in Korea in 2004.[3] BNU now offers a special master's degree program to train teachers in teaching Chinese as second language. BNU has established Confucius institutes in the U.S. in cooperation with the University of Oklahoma and San Francisco State University.

The fourth trend is that Sino-foreign joint schools and programs have grown rapidly. The government developed a basic policy to encourage foreign academics, programs and institutions to offer services in China: "Chinese-foreign cooperation in running schools is an undertaking beneficial to public interests and forms a component of China's educational cause." The number of jointly run programs has grown rapidly, from 70 in 1995 to 1,111 by the end of 2004, representing a 15-fold increase and covering all of China's provinces/autonomous regions/municipalities except Tibet, Ningxia and Gansu. The United States has been the largest partner in joint programs and institutions. BNU now runs an International United College together with Hong Kong Baptist University in Zhuhai, one of China's special economic zones, which brings together 2,200 students from China, Hong Kong, Macau, Taiwan, Korea, the United Kingdom, France, Nigeria and Mali. The students get HKBU degrees when they graduate.

Lessons and Challenges in Developing Sino-U.S. Exchange Relations in Higher Education

Since the first Chinese scholars were sent to the U.S., there have been high and low tides in U.S.-China higher education exchange. But in today's context of rapid change and globalization, neither China nor the U.S. can afford low tides. Both sides must understand each other better and explore new ways to cooperate in higher education. We need to learn from past experiences and meet challenges creatively.

First, we need to lay a solid foundation of mutual cultural understanding for exchange relations. China has thousands of years of civilization, and over this long history it has developed a very strong national identity. But from the mid-19th to mid-20th century, China also experienced humiliation when the world powers invaded and controlled the country. With this cultural burden on their shoulders, Chinese people, especially young people, sometimes react strongly to issues involving relations with the west. Many Chinese people, especially those with educational experiences in the U.S., tend to admire American culture and institutions. But their deep national pride can surface when conflicts appear between China and western countries. While China has been getting stronger, people still have the national psychology of a weak country. For many people, the humiliation that the Chinese people suffered has not receded from their hearts. When we discuss an agreement with western universities, we persistently express the importance of equal rights for both sides. But we often sense arrogance among elite American universities, even if this arrogance is expressed unconsciously. They often lead the discussion, insist on sticking to their plans, and fail to be sufficiently flexible in negotiations. Students and professors who come from the

U.S. are often very critical of what they see and experience, and we do not understand why these elite universities do not show a more positive attitude in establishing exchange relations.

BNU and one of the Ivy League universities have developed a very productive relation in Chinese language and culture education, but not without experiencing conflicts and collisions. The American side assumed control of the program, and treated it as they would any program at their home campus. But we saw it as a cooperative program, and had to have a say in how the program was operated. As we first began to negotiate the program, we could not understand why the other side insisted on selecting textbooks and instructors by themselves and according to their own standards. When they selected articles critical to China's policies or political system for their textbook, the authorities at BNU were under pressure to intervene in the selection, but the American university would not budge from its position. In discussion after discussion, both sides showed their willingness to keep the program going, and gradually began to understand each other's philosophy and ways of thinking. We came to understand that criticism and independent thinking are essential to American culture, and that academic freedom is the very essence of the university. I believe they also began to understand why Chinese people are quite sensitive toward criticism. We learned from this program that students should be at the center of instruction, and we also learned new methods of teaching Chinese as second language. The American side appreciated that BNU had provided the best possible conditions for the program, and it continues to operate well today.

Second, we need to have a strategic way of thinking about brain drain, which will continue to be a major influence on higher educational exchange between China and the U.S. in the foreseeable future. The Chinese government and universities have made tremendous efforts to attract their students back from western countries, but a great proportion of students remain in the U.S. after their studies. At one time, the Chinese government thought that sending advanced scholars would be a good way to guarantee that a high proportion would return, since scholars far along in their careers have more incentive to return to China, but it was later discovered that these scholars often lacked strong motivation to learn. So, the policy pendulum swung back to support study abroad for graduate students. Project 985, a national initiative to support the development of world-class universities in China, provides grants for graduate students to study abroad, and last year there were a dozen of graduate students at BNU who received such grants. This year there will be more, and this will be a regular practice as long as the project runs. I believe this problem can be solved only as China continues to develop and provide better working and living conditions, and universities and governments place more value on academic freedom and academic autonomy.

Third, we need to reconsider the problem of language from an international perspective. As economic globalization accelerates, English is becoming a true international language. As we know, English is the major international language in the academic world, and Chinese universities encourage their faculty members to teach and publish in English. Today, the most popular subjects for Chinese college students are English and computer science, and in general, scholars who return from the U.S. all can communicate in English to varying degrees. Chinese universities welcome international students as a way to make the campus look more international, but at the same time most universities provide separate living quarters for international students, both to show hospitality and to restrain the influence of western values. The level of interaction between Chinese and international students is often relatively low. Most American students now come to China to learn the Chinese language and culture, but strangely enough they often complain that Chinese universities do not offer a wide enough selection of courses in English. Perhaps American young people learn to view English as the natural international language, but they should understand that without mastering a local language they cannot really understand local people. To know a language is to open a window onto a beautiful and colorful world, and English may not be the dominant "international language" forever.

Fourth, we need to overcome bureaucracy to further U.S.-China exchange in higher education. When we talk about bureaucracy, American scholars and students in Chinese universities tend to have a lot to say. It is true that we have a strong bureaucratic government system. Along with higher education reform, Chinese universities have gained great autonomy, and now have the power to sign agreements with overseas universities. Yet, there is no denying that Chinese universities are still subject to the influence of government policy on international affairs. When we discuss exchange with American state universities, we sometimes feel as if they are part of state governments. They lack flexibility and stick to state rules, especially those related to finance. We feel that they do not even have the power and autonomy from government that we enjoy. It is much easier to deal with American private universities. The university has become more accountable to the state as the government has tightened regulations on university use of public funds, but the university must also defend its academic autonomy. Dealing with bureaucracy will be a major challenge for both sides.

Fifth, we need to recognize that market forces are now important in the context of higher education. Higher education institutions compete globally to provide education and research services on a commercial basis.[4] There is no real competition between elite American universities and Chinese universities, but those less prestigious American universities and even some degree mills come to China to compete for students and establish joint degree programs or new institutions. Chinese universities also compete among themselves to attract international students, and some universities lower their admission standards to attract more students. We cannot really escape market forces, but we must meet their challenges creatively while maintaining the core academic values of the university.

Sixth, we need to review existing agreements between Chinese and American universities. Most major Chinese universities have signed quite a few agreements with

American universities, but many of these remain on paper only and no real exchange ever happens. In contrast with this phenomenon, cooperation between individual professors occurs all the time, but usually does not last long. Though the friendship between individual professors may remain forever, their academic cooperation usually does not have a campus-wide influence. We need to include cooperation between individual professors in our institutional agreements and give them support. We need to find out why some agreements work and others do not. Our experience at BNU has been that a program goes well if a dedicated person is responsible for it from beginning to end. If he or she leaves a program, the program tends to have problems. We have found that American program leaders sometimes regard the program as their "baby." So the program has an institutional leader or "champion," but it depends too much on that person.

Last but not least, financial support for higher education exchange relations has always been a challenge. Though we all agree that exchange is important in order for higher education to equip citizens with international understanding and cultural tolerance, governments and higher education institutions must provide continuous financial support to the exchange in order for these benefits to be realized.

Concluding Remarks

Internationalization of higher education is an irreversible trend, and China must participate in it while keeping its cultural traditions and showing the rest of the world that Chinese cultural traditions can contribute to the global knowledge system. If China wants its voice to be heard, it must improve its higher education system to meet international standards. To survive in this interdependent world, a country must be very careful not to fall into narrow nationalism or national nihilism.

Chinese universities have benefitted from the perspective gained through exchange with the U.S., most importantly through feedback from Chinese students returning from the U.S. Chinese universities have made great progress in developing exchange with American universities, as more than 100,000 Chinese students have already returned from the U.S. These returnees have made Chinese universities more open, and Chinese institutions have taken steps to move from the periphery to the center of the international academic world. I believe that more American people read Chinese and understand Chinese culture as a result of these exchange relations, and that both sides have benefited. We must learn from past experiences and meet the challenges for further development of exchange relations between Chinese and American universities.

NOTES

[1] Kathryn Mohrman (Fulbright Scholar, 2002-2003, Chinese University of Hong Kong, Hong Kong America Center), "Higher Education Reform in Mainland Chinese Universities: An American's Perspective," July 2003, 86.

[2] www.moe.edu.cn/edoas/website18/53/info13253.htm.

[3] www.hanban.org/cn_hanban/kzxy.php.

[4] OECD Centre for Educational Research and Innovation, "Four Future Scenarios for Higher Education." Available online: www.oecd.org/dataoecd/22/22/38073691.pdf.

About the Contributors

David B. J. Adams is the Assistant Director for Asia and the Pacific at the Council for International Exchange of Scholars (CIES), a division of the Institute of International Education, where he oversees the program staff that administer Fulbright Scholar Programs in East, Central and South Asia in addition to his own portfolio of programs in East and South Asia, including China. He served as Senior Program Officer at CIES from 1986 to early 2008. From 1998 to 2002 he was the Assistant Director of the ASIA Fellows Program (AFP), which provides opportunities for young Asian scholars to study or do research in another part of Asia. Before becoming an international education administrator, he was a full-time faculty member at the University of Denver, Benedictine College, and Hampden-Sydney College. He received his Ph.D. and M.A. in Political Science from the University of Chicago and his A.B. in government from the College of William and Mary.

Peggy Blumenthal is the Executive Vice President and Chief Operating Officer at the Institute of International Education. In the 1970s, Blumenthal was actively involved in the development of U.S.-China exchanges, as a staff member of the National Committee on U.S.-China Relations and the Asia Society's China Council. She is the author of several works on this subject, including "American Study Programs in China: An Interim Report Card" and "American Study in China: A Half-Open Door." More recent publications include a co-edited volume, *Academic Mobility in a Changing World: Regional and Global Trends* and "An Overview of Cultural and Educational Exchanges" (a co-authored essay in *Transnational Competence: Rethinking the U.S.-Japan Educational Relationship*). She received her B.A. in Modern Chinese History from Harvard University and her M.A. in American Studies from the University of Hawaii at Manoa.

Dana S. Bourgerie is an Associate Professor of Chinese at Brigham Young University. He earned his PhD in East Asian Languages, Chinese linguistics focus, in 1991 from The Ohio State University. Professor Bourgerie has served as a visiting lecturer at Hong Kong City University and at Nanjing University, as well as a Fulbright Fellow at the Chinese University of Hong Kong. His research interests are in language variation, sociolinguistics, Chinese dialect studies, and language acquisition. He has been involved in computer-assisted language instruction for more than fifteen years and has published software for learning Mandarin and Cantonese. Professor Bourgerie is currently serving as the director of the Chinese Flagship Program at BYU and has worked with BYU overseas programs in China and Southeast Asia since 1993. He is past president of the Chinese Language Teachers Association and has served on numerous other national professional and editorial boards.

Carl Falsgraf is Director of the Center for Applies Second Language Studies (CASLS) and the Chinese K-16 Flagship. He holds a doctorate in linguistics, and he has been teaching and conducting research on language education for over twenty years. His classroom experience includes teaching ESL, Japanese, and a variety of graduate courses in pedagogy and methodology. Falsgraf served on the American Council on the Teaching of Foreign Languages Executive Board and as president for the Pacific Northwest Council for Languages. His interests include proficiency assessment, standards-based approaches to language education, and data-driven professional development.

Thomas A. Farrell was named by President George W. Bush as Deputy Assistant Secretary for Academic Programs in May 2002. In this capacity, he is responsible for all academic programs sponsored by the Department of State; these include the Fulbright Program for students, teachers, scholars and mid-career professionals in the Humphrey program, teacher exchange programs, English Language Programs, Study of the United States Programs, and programs for undergraduate students. He serves as the Department of State's lead executive for programs and initiatives such as President Bush's National Security Language Initiative to promote quality teaching and mastery of critical need foreign languages. Farrell came to the Department of State with fourteen years of experience in the private, non-governmental arena that was concentrated on education, professional development, training, and exchange. In 1987, he joined the Institute of International Education (IIE) as Regional Director in Houston, Texas. He was promoted to Vice President of IIE and transferred to New York in 1990, and assigned to Washington, D.C. in 1992.

Margot E.. Landman is Senior Director for Education Programs at the National Committee on United States – China Relations. She had the good fortune to begin studying Chinese in high school with a terrific teacher. At Brown University, she continued her language studies, added Asian history, and then was among the first Americans to go to China to teach after diplomatic recognition in 1979. Since her return to the U.S. in 1982, she has worked in educational and cultural exchange between the U.S. and China, and Asia more broadly, at the university and pre-collegiate levels. She joined the American Council of Learned Societies in 1995 to develop the U.S.-China Teachers Exchange Program, a new program for K-12 teachers generously funded by the Freeman Foundation. She and the program moved to the National Committee on United States – China Relations in 2002. Landman continues to administer the Teachers Exchange Program, as well as other educational programs at the National Committee.

Shepherd Laughlin is a Program Coordinator at IIE's New York headquarters. He has researched and written on U.S.-China educational exchange since joining IIE, and produced a report for the Fund for the Improvement of Postsecondary Education (FIPSE), *Opportunities and Challenges in U.S.-China Educational Linkages*. His senior thesis, *Global China, Local Chinas: Modernization and Ethnic Identity in the People's Republic*, was selected for publication in 2007 by the Brown University Senior Honors Thesis Publication Competition. In 2005, Laughlin traveled to Beijing on a Freeman-ASIA scholarship to study Mandarin. He holds an A.B. in International Relations from Brown University.

Charlotte S. Mason is a Director of The China Exchange Initiative (CEI), formed in 1996 and funded by the Freeman Foundation to create exchange programs, educational partnerships, and administrator shadowing projects between schools in the U.S. and China. In 2000, Mason co-chaired the National Commission for Asia in the Schools, sponsored by the Asia Society with co-chairs Governor James Hunt of North Carolina and Chancellor Chan Lin Tien of the University of California. Mason came to CEI after a long teaching career at Newton (MA) North High School. She was an exchange teacher at the Beijing Jingshan School in 1989. Upon her return, she co-chaired with Carolyn Henderson, also of Newton, the Newton-Beijing Jingshan School Exchange Program, which was founded in 1979 and which continues to thrive. In 2004, she was part of a group of education, business and policy leaders who launched GEM (Global Education Massachusetts), an effort to promote global education in Massachusetts.

Madelyn Ross is currently Director of China Initiatives at George Mason University, where she works with the Office of the Provost to coordinate China-related activities at Mason and develop campus-wide educational initiatives in China. She has also worked as an independent consultant to Asia-focused organizations and projects, and spent nine years at The U.S.-China Business Council, where she was editor of *The China Business Review* and Executive Director of The China Business Forum, a subsidiary of the Council. She is currently a member of the Board of Directors of The China Business Forum and has served as a member of the Advisory Council for the East Asian Studies Department at Princeton University. Ross holds an M.A. in International Affairs from Columbia University and a B.A. in East Asian Studies from Princeton University. She also studied at Fudan University in Shanghai, and has lived and worked in Hong Kong, China, and Taiwan.

Wang Yingjie is a Professor of Education at School of Education, Beijing Normal University (BNU), where he has also been dean and vice-president. He has worked as a visiting scholar at Stanford University, Harvard University (with a Fulbright research scholarship), University of Vermont, University of Trento (Italy) and University of Education of Naruto (Japan). He is a panel chair of the Academic Degree Committee of the State Council, and a vice-president of the National Comparative Education Society. Wang serves as an alternate member of the Governing Board for the UNESCO Institute for Lifelong Learning. His research interests include comparative higher education, higher education administration and policy analysis. His writings involve both academic findings and policy recommendations for educational authorities. He is a member of editorial boards of several academic journals, and has completed joint research projects with scholars from the U.S., the UK, Japan and other countries.

Yang Xinyu joined the Ministry of Education of the People's Republic of China in 1986 after graduating from Heilongjiang University with a B.A. in English Language and Literature. She studied at Nottingham University from 1988-1989 under a British Council scholarship and got her Master of Education in 1989. Yang worked in the Ministry as Senior Program Officer until 1995, when she was appointed Second Secretary for Education in the Chinese Embassy in Canada. She joined China Scholarship Council in 1998 as Deputy Director, and later Director of the Division of Study Abroad Affairs. She took the position as the Deputy Secretary-General of CSC in 2003.

IIE-Administered Study Abroad Scholarships and Resources

OPEN DOORS REPORT ON INTERNATIONAL EDUCATIONAL EXCHANGE
The Open Doors Report on International Educational Exchange, supported by the U.S. Department of State Bureau of Educational and Cultural Affairs, provides a long-standing, comprehensive statistical analysis of academic mobility between the United States and the nations of the world.

WEBSITE: www.opendoors.iienetwork.org

IIE STUDY ABROAD WHITE PAPER SERIES: MEETING AMERICA'S GLOBAL EDUCATION CHALLENGE
IIE launched a new policy research initiative to address the issue of capacity abroad, in order to help pave the way for substantial study abroad growth.

Current Trends in U.S. Study Abroad & the Impact of Strategic Diversity Initiatives (May 2007)
Exploring Host Country Capacity for Increasing U.S. Study Abroad (May 2008)
Expanding Education Abroad at U.S. Community Colleges (September 2008)

WEBSITE: www.iie.org/StudyAbroadCapacity

IIE BRIEFING PAPERS
IIE Briefing Papers are a rapid response to the changing landscape of international education, offering timely snapshots of critical issues in the field.

Educational Exchange between the United States and China (July 2008)

WEBSITE: www.iie.org/researchpublications

IIEPASSPORT.ORG
This free online search engine lists over 8,000 study abroad programs worldwide and provides advisers with hands-on tools to counsel students and promote study abroad.

WEBSITE: www.iiepassport.org

STUDY ABROAD FUNDING
This valuable funding resource helps U.S. students find funding for their study abroad.

WEBSITE: www.studyabroadfunding.org

Funding Opportunities for U.S. Students & Scholars

FULBRIGHT PROGRAMS

FULBRIGHT PROGRAMS FOR U.S. STUDENTS
SPONSOR: U.S. Department of State, Bureau of Educational and Cultural Affairs
DEADLINE: October
WEBSITE: http://us.fulbrightonline.org

FULBRIGHT PROGRAMS FOR U.S. SCHOLARS
SPONSOR: U.S. Department of State, Bureau of Educational and Cultural Affairs
DEADLINE: August, November, February
CONTACT: apprequest@cies.iie.org; Tel: 202-686-4000
WEBSITE: www.cies.org

BENJAMIN A. GILMAN INTERNATIONAL SCHOLARSHIP PROGRAM
SPONSOR: U.S. Department of State, Bureau of Educational and Cultural Affairs
DEADLINE: April and October
CONTACT: gilman@iie.org; Tel: 713-621-6300, ext 25
WEBSITE: www.iie.org/gilman

NSEP PROGRAMS

DAVID L. BOREN SCHOLARSHIPS & FELLOWSHIPS
SPONSOR: National Security Education Program
DEADLINE: January and February
CONTACT: boren@iie.org; Tel: 800-618-NSEP
WEBSITE: www.borenawards.org

THE LANGUAGE FLAGSHIP FELLOWSHIPS
SPONSOR: National Security Education Program
DEADLINE: January
CONTACT: flagship@iie.org; Tel: 800-618-NSEP
WEBSITE: www.flagshipfellowships.org

FREEMAN-ASIA: AWARDS FOR STUDY IN ASIA
SPONSOR: Freeman Foundation
DEADLINE: March, April and October
CONTACT: Freeman-Asia@iie.org; Tel: 212-984-5542
WEBSITE: www.iie.org/Freeman-Asia

WHITAKER INTERNATIONAL FELLOWS AND SCHOLARS PROGRAM
SPONSOR: Whitaker Foundation
DEADLINE: January
CONTACT: whitaker@iie.org; Tel: 212-984-5442
WEBSITE: www.whitakerawards.org